SMART TART

FORTNUM & MASON

PICCADILLY SINCE 1707

SMART TART

....

OBSERVATIONS FROM MY COOKING LIFE

....

Tamasin Day-Lewis

unbound

ABOUT THE AUTHOR

Tamasin Day-Lewis is a writer and film-maker who has now written more than a dozen books including *The Art of the Tart*, *Tamasin's Kitchen Bible*, *Tamasin's Kitchen Classics*, *Tarts with Tops On*, *Good Tempered Food*, *West of Ireland Summers* and *Where Shall We Go for Dinner?* She has also directed and produced 28 documentaries for the BBC, ITV and Channel 4 and hosted two TV cooking series. She appears regularly as a commentator on the radio and writes about the arts for American *Vanity Fair*. She contributes to numerous magazines and newspapers on subjects related and unrelated to food. She lives mainly in her kitchen, which is in Somerset, County Mayo, London and the houses of her friends, where she usually ends up cooking dinner.

This limited edition printed exclusively
for Fortnum & Mason in 2013.

This edition first published in 2013.

Unbound, 4–7 Manchester Street,
Marylebone, London, W1U 2AE
www.unbound.co.uk

The extract from 'Figs' by D.H.
Lawrence was taken from *Birds, Beasts
& Flowers*, first published by Martin
Secker (London) in 1923 and in this
version from the Penguin Classics
edition of the *Selected Poems*, edited by
James Fenton (2008) and reproduced by
permission of Pollinger Limited and the
Estate of Frieda Lawrence Ravagli.

Design and typeset by Tappin Gofton
Cover design by Mecob
Photography by Robert Fairer
Illustration by John Broadley

A CIP record for this book is available
from the British Library

ISBN 978-1-78352-015-2
(trade edn)
ISBN 978-1-78352-016-9
(limited edn)
ISBN 978-1-78352-014-5
(ebook edn)
ISBN 978-1-78352-023-7
(Fortnum & Mason edn)

Print Producion
Arnold Moon Ltd

'Dwell on the beauty of life. Watch the stars, and see yourself running with them.'

'Never forget that the universe is a single living organism possessed of one substance and one soul, holding all things suspended in a single consciousness and creating all things with a single purpose that they might work together spinning and weaving and knotting whatever comes to pass.'

Marcus Aurelius, *Meditations*, (AD 121–180)

At Fortnum & Mason, we have been in the business of pleasure since 1707 and I cannot think of anything more pleasurable than the first bite into a warm fruit tart, topped with cool crème anglaise, on a summer's day.

With its marriage of flavours, its beguiling combination of textures, the juxtaposition of smooth and silky filling with crumbly shortcrust pastry, the possibilities are endless. This is not the humble tart. This is the king of baked items.

Tamasin has been coming to Fortnum's since she was a child. She enjoyed scones, finger sandwiches, cakes and, of course, tarts with her grandmother and her brother at the Fountain Restaurant, where we serve our famous tea. Tamasin told me that these early experiences piqued her interest in food and so it's a real honour that she has repaid Fortnum's and our customers with this special edition of *Smart Tart*.

I hope you enjoy baking tarts from Tamasin's book in your home, and joining us at the Fountain Restaurant, in our home, for a tart made by one of our fine pastry chefs.

Ewan Venters
CEO, Fortnum & Mason

CONTENTS

1 BAKEWELL TART 3

2 TEA AT FORTNUM'S FOUNTAIN 13

3 CHRISTMAS 35

4 THE THINGS I LOVE AND THE THINGS I HATE ABOUT FOOD 47

5 TREACLE TART 61

6 SLOWLY COOKED 71

7 CHILDHOOD TARTS 85

8 HOMESTART 101

9 THE PARTICULAR SPOT 115

10 REVOLUTION 129

11 FIGS 149

12 FAMINE 163

13 MATTERS OF THE HEART 175

14 THE BEST RESTAURANT 189

1 BAKEWELL TART

Rhoda Fisher was my grandparents' cook in the days when cooks were cooks not chefs: they lived in, were 'in service', it was a job for life. Rhoda retired well into her seventies after a lifetime of routine. Of appearing in my grandfather's dressing room first thing each morning to discuss the menu for the day with my grandmother. Of agreeing to cook exactly what was asked of her six days a week.

I still have an old black and white photograph of me sitting on Rhoda's knee on the low wall that surrounded the drive at Upper Parrock, my grandparents' house. Me as a toddler, Rhoda in her old maid's shoes: black, laced high up the instep; hair netted and scraped tight into a tiny grey bun; her clothes always careful not to draw attention to themselves: maroon cardigans, navy blue, modest, clean, carefully pressed; moderate in her words and deeds; her room, the little bedroom next to the four-poster room that my brother Dan slept in when we went to stay; shared bathroom, a home, but not – oh never – her home.

My earliest tart memory, other than the jam tarts I helped make in my mother's kitchen, where the molten jam welded itself to the roof of your mouth in the agony of greed and haste that meant the never-cooling-what-you'd-cooked of childhood, was Rhoda's Bakewell. It is almost the memory of a memory so faint is the whiff of bitter almonds and her home-made bubbling, seedy raspberry jam seeping into the frangipane. Not that I knew the word then. The shortest of pastries, the most brown-buttery scented, nutty middle; the contrast of hot sweet jam with sticky almond.

Perhaps the pleasure for Rhoda was seeing the tart sent out to the dining room, and the tart tin returned as picked clean as a skull. The cream came out of the silver jug in clots you couldn't control and began to turn to butter on the slice. The jam oozed and wept. We never tired of this simple classic. It became, with lemon meringue pie and treacle tart, one of the defining puddings of childhood, of Upper Parrock, of my grandparents' polished table, the oak whorled and stained and contoured with the age and weight of dinners gone by over nearly two centuries.

My Bakewell tastes nothing like Rhoda's, how could it? I grind Marcona almonds from Spain's southern groves and intensify them with a smidge of bitter almond. My jam could never taste as good as the warm raspberries I picked there in the Sussex walled kitchen garden, because the food of childhood still has newness and surprise attached to it. My pastry is just different, like everyone else's always is. My tart is less cakey-middled, more damp. But the funny thing is, every time I make a Bakewell tart I don't try to recreate Rhoda's but I involuntarily recreate the memory of it. I am swept back to the table where the happiest meals of my childhood took place – other than in the west of Ireland – and to the quiet gentlewoman whose life was measured not in coffee spoons, but in the approval and joy of others that is the pleasure of any generous-hearted cook.

......................:...................

Opposite top, Tamasin with her grandparents
Opposite bottom, Tamasin with Rhoda Fisher

BAKEWELL TART

I bother to buy lovely Spanish Marcona almonds and grind them myself for this dish, for flavour and texture. Ready-ground almonds are invariably dry and stale, but do what you will. Home-made raspberry jam, or the best you can find please, so that you have whole raspberries and seediness. You may prefer apricot, blackcurrant or strawberry jam. I also sliver my own almonds to scatter on top after cooking, tossing them in a little hot pan for just long enough over the heat for them to begin to release their oil and turn biscuit-coloured.

300g best raspberry jam
150g unsalted butter
120g vanilla caster sugar
200g whole skinned almonds or ground almonds
3 eggs + 1 yolk
1 tsp bitter almond extract
3 heaped tbsp double cream
a handful of whole skinned almonds to sliver and toast

makes 20 cm/8 inch tart
serves 6–8

Preheat oven to 180°C/Gas 4. Make shortcrust pastry (see p.196) and line a 20 cm/8 inch tart tin. Bake blind and return to the oven in the usual way.

Heat the raspberry jam with 1 tsp water gently until warm and runny. Heat the butter in a small pan and when it has melted, allow it to cook until it has just turned brown and started to smell nutty.

Pour the brown butter over the sugar, ground almonds, beaten eggs and yolk, double cream and bitter almond extract which you have stirred together in a bowl. Mix together.

When you remove the tart from its 10 minutes drying out in the oven after baking blind, pour over the jam, scrape on the filling and return to the middle shelf of the oven for between 35–40 minutes. The top should be browned and set. Remove to a rack.

Dry fry the flaked almonds, a handful, until biscuity and oily and sprinkle over the top. Allow to cool for at least 15 minutes before turning out and serving with clotted cream.

Note: This frangipane mixture works well with a cherry and almond tart, so make it in exactly the same way adding 3–4 dozen stoned cherries to the mixture in the summer, or 400g drained morello cherries from a jar in the winter.

TEA AT FORTNUM'S FOUNTAIN

2 TEA AT FORTNUM'S FOUNTAIN

The food you experience in childhood always remains the food you return to for succour and comfort. Obviously I am not referring to school food here. Things like the pudding we christened 'Purple Puke' that we imagined grew under the school quad and Manchester tart, which was a heinous concoction of grey margarined pastry, turnip jam, cornfloury custard and a dusting of toenails on top, the hideous, desiccated coconut flakes that stuck in teeth and craw.

But those earliest taste memories are really not about expensive, luxurious ingredients. They are about the simplest of things that make home seem like home: eggy bread for breakfast with a lacey frill of egg around the more squelchy, golden middle; airy puffballs of Yorkshire pudding with bloody gravy from the beef sogging into them on the plate; the first sweet peas from the garden drowning in cream and butter and mint; crumpets with far too much butter; soggy fat chips doused in watered down malt vinegar and salt from the chip shop where I changed buses on the way home from school; vanilla ice cream with chocolate sauce poured on top that sets as you watch it like ice on a pond, the ice cream turning to milky liquid; doughnuts with a burst of jam, doughy-middled and crisp skinned, the sugar gritting your mouth and teeth.

We don't think about texture when we are young, but there it is, assaulting our taste buds and palate like a fist, its contrasts affording us such sensual pleasure as they play into each others' hands: crisp with soft; mallowy with custardy; crunch and grit with silken, slippery and gelled. Our senses delight in things that stick to our teeth, our tongues, the roofs of our mouths; that feast the eye with colour, the nose with scent, that alert us to almost-pleasure and activate our taste buds.

Is the real thing, the first bite, ever as exciting as the anticipation, the expectation, the wait?

Is the childhood memory in later life not best of all? The reminder of when treats were treats and became, with repetition – but not too often – tradition and ritual, defined our family and its particularity and singularity from everyone else's?

What was, and remains, the best treat of my childhood – my mind is still stirred to pleasure by it and, when I conjure it up, I remember it with a smile, a taste – was my trips to Fortnum's Fountain for tea with my grandmother.

My maternal grandmother took more pride and joy in keeping a good table than many in her social position during those times where having a cook and staff and a kitchen garden and home farm were not as unusual as they are now. Hers was not an era of food and restaurant culture, but, being well travelled and cultured in the European sense, she brought her knowledge to her kitchen and thence to the dining room.

When she was not in the country house in Sussex with my grandfather, she was in a dark, quite gloomy flat in Mayfair's Down Street. 'You can only go up Down Street,' she used to say, deposited there on a Monday morning with eggs and cream from the country by her chauffeur Shackleton in the beetle-black shiny Bentley.

I hated it, I felt sick in the ridged leather seats that Dan and I sat in on the journey down to Sussex with our nanny for holidays, and I was, invariably, sick on the journey. Thank God in London we walked, though walking was not an activity my grandmother indulged in much in London or the country. Except to 'the little grocer's down the road', Fortnum's.

As my brother Dan and I were swirled in through the doors, the red tailcoated assistants would welcome my grandmother with a 'Good afternoon m'lady' and we would idle past the riveting tins of bees in honey and ants in chocolate, imagining what they tasted like, and downstairs into the embrace of the Fountain.

The waitresses, in those days, were there for the duration and changed as rarely as the uniforms and the menu. That was the point. Something that modern restaurateurs and chefs singularly fail to grasp, is that many of us return for the comfort of sameness. And in our case, we never ventured off-piste. We would have been to the dentist first, our great-uncle Gerald in Devonshire Place, but, far from being afeared, we knew that next stop was Fortnum's, so the whole trip was a treat.

We ordered freshly squeezed orange juice, chocolate Sachertorte and blackcurrant ice cream which came in a heavy sundae glass with a squirl of whipped cream and a thick fan wafer. Sometimes Dan had a Dusty Road which had, I seem to remember, a rubble of chocolate and blackcurrants in syrup poured around the ice cream and little shards of broken meringue. Children's heaven. Our grandmother would beam indulgently. I think she got as much pleasure from watching us eat as she did from eating. If we didn't want a second helping she would ask us if we were sickening for something. When did a child *not* want more ice cream?

Fortnum's Sachertorte thrills and surprises each time. Like mercury, it slips through your fingers evanescently when you try to define it. It's partly the gleaming bitter chocolate on top with its hidden, sharp-apricot glaze that the chocolate cake crumb absorbs beneath, and the strata of thick, rich chocolate that break the layers of sponge and seems to burst onto the roof of your mouth. But really it is the whole thing, not too sweet or too tart, that just does it for me.

The purists who insist chocolate is best left to itself and not adulterated by fruit simply fail to understand the point. Apricots, cherries and raspberries were born to work with chocolate if you get the balance and the sweetness right. Shunning a Black Forest gâteau as suburban kitsch misses the point. It's all about technique and ingredients.

I use Julian Temperley's morello cherry eau de vie and his jars of morello cherries that he sells dunked in eau de vie in my chocolate brownie tart and the principle is the same, the very essence of cherriness with their whiff of bitter almonds buried in bitter chocolate. If you get the texture right you have that raw-looking un-crumby brownie texture that squidges moreishly in the mouth.

If you can't be bothered to make pastry just make the brownies: who is going to know you've only made the middle of the recipe?

But the tart really is a treat. Just like Fortnum's Fountain.

....

CHOCOLATE AND CHERRY BROWNIE TART

This is a humdinger of a tart, which I make with fresh cherries in the summer, and a jar of morello cherries in the winter, soaked in Julian Temperley's cherry eau de vie, which can be skipped by the faint-hearted. The crimson, almondy, cherry whiff embedded in the sludgy, giving, depths of brownie is quite enough, in fact all it takes, to radiate happiness.

3–4 dozen cherries, stoned and soaked in
2 tbsp cherry eau de vie, or cognac with a few drops of bitter almond essence
200g dark chocolate, Valrhona le Noir 68% is the best, keep 50g for the top
250g unsalted butter
4 eggs
150g each light muscovado and vanilla caster sugar
1 tsp vanilla extract
120g plain or '00' flour
a level tsp baking powder
a pinch of sea salt
2 tbsp dark cocoa powder, like Green & Black's
a few brace of cherries to decorate the top

makes 26 cm/10 inch tart
serves 8–10

Preheat oven to 180°C/Gas 4. Make sweet crust pastry with 180g/90g ratio (see p.198). Bake blind in 26 cm/10 inch tart tin and dry out in the usual way. Meanwhile, make the brownie mix and soak the cherries.

Melt the chocolate and butter together gently in a pan over a low heat and remove from the heat before the chocolate is all liquid, so it doesn't separate. Cool. Beat the eggs, sugars and vanilla with the Kitchen Aid or mixer whisk until really light and considerably thickened, which will take 2–3 minutes.

Sift in the flour, baking powder, salt and cocoa powder, scrape in the chocolate and butter and beat briefly to combine. Remove the cup from the mixer and add the stoned cherries in their liquor with a rubber spatula, folding them in, then scrape the mixture into the pastry case, smooth and return to the oven to bake for 35–40 minutes.

A skewer should come out a little sticky, but not coated with liquid chocolate.

Remove to a rack and cool until warm. Turn out the brownie tart. Warm the rest of the chocolate very gently and then dip in a few pairs of cherries and place them on top of the tart. Drip melted chocolate over the tart. Serve warm, room temperature, or chilled – though the texture is much more fudgy when cold – with Jersey or clotted cream. And a shot of cherry eau de vie.

JAM OR CURD TARTS

There are three ways to make these simplest of tarts, two of which, to my mind, work best, but it is all a matter of taste.

If you bake the jam with the pastry it will bubble Vesuvially, which may be what you like, up and over the pastry rims. It will also taste cooked.

Alternatively, you can cook the pastry cases first, then add the heated jams when the cases come out of the oven.

The third way, my preferred way, which gives you a rawer, more intense flavour, is to cook the pastry then plop in the jam. It glistens seductively, you can pile in more with no fear of it erupting, and the tarts taste really fruity.

These traffic light tarts are the way to go, no child doesn't want to choose a colour, then another, then another.

Fortnum's delectable curds shouldn't be cooked, they are cooked, so they should be added to the cooked pastry. Best chilled too. The raspberry curd is my tart, tart favourite, then the rhubarb, but the lemon and the lime are both divine.

Roll out 180g/190g pastry and cut out 2 dozen little tarts, pushing them into the greased tart tins.

Prick the bottoms and edges with a fork and brush lightly with beaten egg for colour and crispness. Bake for 12–15 minutes at 180°C/Gas 4 then remove to a rack and plop on the jams and curds.

LEMON CURD AND PASSION FRUIT CURD

Fortnum's have a golden raspberry, a woodland strawberry and a blackcurrant jam that are the scent of summer, such a treat. I have also made a lime marmalade tart for a touch of green, so you really can eat three traffic light colours.

Home-made curds are thrillingly easy to make, just make sure you use unwaxed citrus fruit, organic is best, unrefined sugar and the best unsalted butter.

. . . .

2 large, organic lemons
90g unsalted butter cut
    into cubes
225g unrefined granulated
    sugar
3 large eggs

. . . .

serves 12

Choose a wide-bottomed saucepan as the curd cooks and gels quicker.

Grate the zest from the lemons, and add it with their juice, the butter and the sugar to the pan.

Stir over a gentle heat until the sugar dissolves; don't let the mixture come to the boil.

Beat the eggs and add them to the mixture then keep stirring and watching the mixture until the curd thickens.

Remove from the heat instantly and scrape into the cooked tart shells.

. . . .

10 large or 14 small
    wrinkly passion fruit
120g unsalted butter
2 large eggs + 3 large yolks
110g unrefined caster
    sugar

. . . .

serves 12

Scoop the flesh from the fruit into a sieve placed over a bowl. Push as much juice through as you can, then decant the contents of the sieve into a small pan and heat gently to warm. Set aside.

Melt the butter in a wide-bottomed pan over a gentle heat then stir in the eggs and sugar and the sieved passion fruit juice from the bowl.

Stir until the mixture thickens, still over a gentle heat, then remove from the heat and sieve over the rest of the pulp from the sieve, adding a dessertspoon of the seeds.

Pour the curd into your baked tart shell or little tart shells.

GAMMON AND SPINACH TART WITH MONTGOMERY'S CHEDDAR AND SEEDED MUSTARD

This tart was inspired by the frog-he-would-a-wooing-go combination of gammon and spinach. I couldn't resist. I decided to pair the rosy pink smoked gammon and dark, leafy green spinach, with two of the most British of ingredients: unpasteurised, aged Somerset Cheddar from Jamie Montgomery and seeded mustard for a little piquancy.

It worked to perfection first time round, so here it is.

300ml carton double or Jersey cream

2 eggs + 2 yolks

1½ dstspns seeded mustard

sea salt and pepper

120g coarsely grated Montgomery or good, unpasteurised aged Cheddar

150g chunk of smoked gammon chopped into small cubes

1 tbsp olive oil

200g organic spinach

makes 24 cm/9½ inch tart serves 8

Preheat the oven to 180°C/Gas 4. Make the shortcrust pastry (see p.196) and bake blind and dry in the oven.

In a large bowl, whisk the cream, eggs, mustard and seasoning together then add the cheese and ham.

Heat the olive oil in a pan and add the washed spinach, stirring for a couple of minutes, just until it wilts.

Press the spinach in a colander to drain the watery green juices out.

Strew the spinach over the base of the pre-baked tart shell, scrape in the filling and bake for 40 minutes or until browned and puffed up and just set.

Remove from the oven to a rack and cool for 15 minutes before turning out and serving.

A lively salad of tomatoes, or of red peppers, asparagus and finely sliced raw fennel, or a little dish of buttered, minted peas make a great accompaniment.

SMOKED SALMON, ARTICHOKE, SOUR CREAM AND CHIVE TART

This is a tart for a feast. So often a smoked salmon tart is an apology for some leftover bits of farmed, greasy, inferior smoked salmon and not much else. I won't touch farmed or organic smoked salmon, I'd rather see the real thing as a treat, less often. So here I used Fortnum's London Cure wild smoked salmon; H. Forman & Son perfected the London cure over 100 years ago and it is not too smoky, not too salt. The salmon is allowed to speak for itself.

So, if you have smoky, salty, fishy, what better than to pair it with baby artichoke hearts that come in a jar of extra virgin olive oil and add earthy piquancy. Sour cream and smoked salmon just work, the cream's lactic sharpness cuts through the salmon's richness, and the chives add an oniony greenness.

This really is a splendid tart that you could serve as easily over the Christmas period as you could at a lovely summer picnic or lunch.

300 ml carton soured cream

150 ml each single and double cream

2 eggs + 3 yolks

white pepper to grind

280g jar baby artichoke hearts in extra virgin olive oil

6 slices wild smoked salmon

1 tbsp snipped chives

makes 24 cm/9½ inch tart
serves 8

Preheat the oven to 180°C/Gas 4. Bake the shortcrust pastry blind in the usual way (see p.196), likewise dry it out.

Whisk together the soured cream and creams with the eggs and yolks and grind over some white pepper. You will not need salt, smoked salmon is salty.

Remove the artichoke hearts from the jar and place them all around the tart shell. Strew the slices of smoked salmon amongst them, gently tearing them into thick, long pieces, a couple per slice.

Pour over the cream and eggs and then scatter over the chives.

Return the tart to the oven to bake, it will take about 40 minutes to just set, puff up and brown.

Remove to a rack and cool for 15 minutes before turning out and serving. Snip over some extra chives for greenness.

Serve with a tomato salad or some minted peas and Jersey new potatoes in the summer.

3 CHRISTMAS

The Christmas Tree
C. Day Lewis

Put out the lights now!
Look at the Tree, the rough tree dazzled
In oriole plumes of flame,
Tinselled with twinkling frost fire, tasselled
With stars and moons – the same
That yesterday hid in the spinney and had no fame
Till we put out the lights now.

Hard are the nights now:
The fields at moonrise turn to agate,
Shadows are cold as jet;
In dyke and furrow, in copse and faggot
The frost's tooth is set;
And stars are the sparks whirled out by the north wind's fret
On the flinty nights now.

So feast your eyes now
On mimic star and moon-cold bauble:
Worlds may wither unseen,
But the Christmas Tree is a tree of fable,
A phoenix in evergreen,
And the world cannot change or chill what its mysteries mean
To your hearts and eyes now.

The vision dies now
Candle by candle: the tree that embraced it
Returns to its own kind,
To be earthed again and weather as best it
May the frost and the wind.
Children, it too had its hour – you will not mind
If it lives or dies now.

The Christmas tree stood on the Broadwood baby grand piano in the drawing room, little metallic shells of candlestick holders filled with squirly, barley-sugar scarlet candles clipped onto the ends of its needled branches and topped with a straw angel that I have inherited. The ritual was that Papa would light the candles on Christmas Eve and the magic of Christmas would begin the moment the match was struck.

Next the lights would be turned off, and, warmed by the coal fire, Dan and I would sit on our father's lap while he read his poem 'The Christmas Tree' to us by candlelight.

Christmas is all about expectation. It is almost, but not quite, a disappointment to the child when the day actually dawns and there is no longer anything to look forward to.

Papa's next ritual was to read Beatrix Potter's *The Tailor of Gloucester* to us. Dan's cat was named after Simpkin, the cat in the tale. Each time Papa got to the passage about the missing 'one more skein of cherry-coloured twist' that the poor tailor, 'worn to a shravel,' needed to complete the embroidered waistcoat he was stitching, my heart would almost break. The tailor went to bed on Christmas Eve sick with worry, believing he was undone, ruined. And when he awoke the mice had completed the waistcoat for him. The suspension of disbelief nothing to the child's mind, and even, years later, to my adult mind when I continued the ritual with my children. The story of Christmas belongs to each and every one of us and how we interpret and tell it to our children is in the gift of our imagination.

But I have never wanted the fairy tale to end. So I have never subscribed to the notion that Christmas is for children. My children see this as an indication, I suspect, that I don't see reality for what it is, that I am 'away with the fairies'. Well, how could I not be? My father encouraged the blurring of the edges of imagination and reality and read the bible of Andrew Lang to us. Lang's fairy stories are allegories; fairy tales are morality tales, they are just not reasoned, they are imagined, so they work their way down through our conscious mind to our unconscious mind and a little bit of their numinousness works its way into the fabric of our soul, if we are lucky enough.

Every morning at breakfast, my father would place a little crust at the edge of his plate and leave it there. I would ask him why he didn't eat it and his reply would be, 'It's for the little people.' As a child it was a tacit invitation to stay in the realms of the imagination but to see it for what it was. It wasn't, like the shock of finding out that Father Christmas wasn't real, about that. It was about keeping the mystery and the life of the imagination alive, of story-telling, of the known translated into the believable, into fiction, where you don't need to know whether the story is about a real-life character, a composite of several, or one who has been dreamt up.

'Is it true?' children cry, and if you're lucky, a parent will say 'Of course it's true.'

That way, you stay on the side of the story-teller whose world is real, you know it is, you enter into it by falling down its rabbit-hole or walking through its wardrobe door.

So, my children have learned to indulge my wanting to enter the story-like world of Christmas anew each year, and banish, in our family at least, the myth that we do it for them. Even though they are 'grown-up' now.

What family doesn't have a spectacular row at some stage over the turkey? And what the hell's wrong with them if they don't? Our unrealistic expectations of The Perfect Day are partly responsible; we won't countenance anything less than that, but all the best laid plans of mice and men! And there are always tears. Age-old battle scars re-surface; tiredness, emotion, drink unleash a family's dissonances. And there is nothing wrong with that. In a curious sort of way, it's the tears that make for the perfect Christmas, it's just our attitude to them that doesn't. The perfection lies in the imperfection.

The Bah humbug curmudgeonliness of the Christmas-hater who sees only his moral superiority for discounting Christmas, snarking about wasting time and money, is the person I feel sorry for. The less of a ritual build-up to the day, the less you will stir the magic into being; and then you will have less of the 'now' that my father refers to at the beginning and end of each stanza of his poem, the repetition and rhythm setting up the expectation, the aliveness, the sense that we must dwell in the 'now' and pluck the day.

It is the very repetition of the word 'now' that we try to recreate each year anyway, the memory of Christmases past – the Ghost of Christmas Past with the Scrooges amongst us – becoming present and, in turn, future, as successive generations re-interpret their family tradition and make it their own.

My three children always measured out the ingredients and stirred the mincemeat and the Christmas pudding when they were small. The excitement of anticipation began on stir-up Sunday at the end of November, though I was frequently late. They punched out pastry circles, stars, moons and Christmas tree shapes for the mince pies and plopped laden teaspoons of the boozy fruited and nutted mixture into the pastry shells. I bought – and still do – a new decoration for the tree each year, but my silver and gold stars and cobwebs made when I was a child come out of the ancient box for the children to constellate the tree with too. As do the old candlestick holders. And even if they only return on Christmas Eve now, decorating the tree is still the children's ritual. The Christmas tree often sits more forlornly awaiting its transformation nowadays than it does when it is de-robed in time to be carried, de-nuding itself further as sprays of needles fall to the ground, to be burnt in the field.

Tweaking tradition is just about permissible, as I discovered last Christmas when I thought stuff the turkey: yes, but I don't want to make mince pies and no-one will eat enough of them anyway. A fridgeful of accusatory jars of mincemeat six months later is all very well, indeed, turning them upside down and adding to their alcohol when I remember has certainly happened over the years. But what about something more original that is still scented with Christmas, with spicy, nutty, citrus notes that will dazzle and sparkle and delight. I dreamed up a Marcona almond and crystallised orange tart, and no-one shrieked 'go back to the original'. Eaten with a dollop of crème fraîche laced with Cointreau it was a minor sensation.

The tart form is perfect for the ravening hordes and impromptu fridge raids by the Viking-appetited children over the ten-day season. Try a thing of substance and address, a sausage tart made with leftover stuffing into which you may stir prunes or apples. Add black pudding if there isn't enough sausage, tomatoes if you want more of a brunchy feel. Plop the cranberry sauce under a shroud of white chocolate and a cocoa crust and you've got a cold, snowy heaven of a tart. Try making passion fruit curd for a joyously scented sense of the Tropics and the sun, or conjure a simple, savoury tart with the end of the Stichelton or Stilton or a red onion squash, sage and goat's cheese tart to beat the meat-fest into submission.

A tart or two up the sleeve at Christmas is a mighty fine thang when the surfeit of richery leaves you gasping for the homely, the comforting, the crowd pleaser.

If my words are unconvincing and you're harbouring a suppressed 'well it's alright for her' rage at the idea that I may have more time or inclination than you to spend on Christmas, well, you're wrong.

The Christmas tree is a symbol in my father's poem:

> ... a tree of fable,
A phoenix in evergreen.

Before 'the vision dies now' consider that each Christmas you have one less, and that the collective spirit you choose to light alongside the tree is a flame that doesn't go out with the tree, it is a phoenix in evergreen. And make a few tarts.

· · · · · · · · · · · · · · · · · · : · · · · · · · · · · · · · · · ·

ALMOND AND CRYSTALLISED ORANGE TART

Make this jewel of a tart with proper halves of crystallised fruit, not the horrid apology of candied fruit. You should find it in any good deli. You may make a St Clement's if you prefer and do half orange, half lemon, though I prefer orange with added zest.

150g unsalted butter
200g whole marcona almonds
3 eggs + 1 yolk
120g light muscovado sugar
1 vanilla pod
1 crystallised orange, ¾ finely chopped for the middle of the tart, ¼ cut into long thin strips for the top
zest of 2 oranges
2 tbsps apricot jam and a tsp water to glaze

makes 26 cm/10 inch tart
serves 8–10

Preheat oven to 180°C/Gas 4. Make and line the tart tin with pâté sucrée or sablée pastry (see p.198), bake blind and dry out.

Meanwhile, make the filling: melt the butter. Grind the almonds in the Magimix so they have a slightly coarse texture.

Put them in a large bowl with the eggs, sugar, scraped out vanilla pod, finely chopped crystallised orange and zest and pour over the melted butter.

Mix together.

Scrape into the tart case and bake until set and golden, 35–40 minutes.

Cool on a rack.

Warm the jam with the water and brush over the warm tart.

Sprinkle over the last quarter of very finely sliced crystallised peel immediately, so that it sticks to the jam.

SAUSAGE TART

An un-temperamental dish that you can make with sausage meat or skinned sausages, to which you can add black pudding if you feel like it in a 50:50 mix, the black centre stage of the tart, the sausage meat edging it.

Fried apples or prunes are equally good, and I like sautéed red onion, celery and sage leaves with the apple.

1 tbsp olive oil
1 large red onion, peeled and chopped
2 eating apples, peeled, quartered and chopped
2 stalks celery, strung and finely chopped
12 or so sage leaves, chopped coarsely
sea salt and pepper
6 good, organic pure pork sausages, skinned
1–2 dstspns seeded or Dijon mustard, whatever your preference

makes 24 cm/9½ inch tart
serves 8

Preheat the oven to 180°C/Gas 4. Make the usual shortcrust pastry (see p.196) and bake blind then dry out in the oven.

Meanwhile, make the filling: heat a frying pan over a medium heat, add the oil when the pan is hot and then slosh in the chopped onion, apples, celery and sage leaves, season and sauté until beginning to turn translucent and soften. Crumble in the sausages and fry a little longer, just to begin browning them.

Remove the tart from the oven and spread the mustard over the base – if you like mustard – then scrape the contents of the pan into the tart shell and pat down gently.

Return to the oven for 35–40 minutes or until browned and cooked through.

If you decide on prunes, use Agen, they are the best, and chop them into the frying pan when you take it off the heat.

Remove from the oven and cool for 15 minutes before turning out and serving.

Great with jacket potatoes and salad or on the beach, cold.

STILTON, CELERY AND RED ONION TART

This doesn't have to be a leftover Christmas Stilton tart. I have just made it in broad July sunshine and eaten it in the garden in the evening, with a little aperitif, a perfect salty foil for a pink drink made with – no, I won't tell you, you will find it in the last chapter and it's called an Edouardini, except mine has gin, not vodka in the mix.

200 ml double cream

2 eggs + 2 yolks

1 tbsp olive oil

30g unsalted butter

2 medium red onions, peeled and thinly sliced

6 celery stalks, with leaves, strung and chopped small

white pepper, the cheese is too salty to need extra

120g good Stilton like Colston Bassett

makes 24 cm/9½ inch tart
serves 6

Preheat the oven to 180°C/Gas 4. Make the shortcrust pastry in the usual way (see p.196), bake blind, dry out.

Meanwhile, make the filling: whisk the cream and eggs together in a large bowl.

Heat the olive oil and butter together in a heavy-bottomed frying pan and when bubbling, add the onion and celery and turn to coat. Put a lid over the pan, turn the heat down and cook gently until softened, about 20 minutes.

Grind over some white pepper.

Crumble the Stilton into the cream and egg mixture.

Remove the tart from the oven and cover the bottom of the pastry with the onion and celery mixture.

Scrape the cream mixture over the top, trying to spread the Stilton evenly.

Return to the oven and bake for about 40 minutes until well browned and puffed up all over.

Cool on a rack for at least 20 minutes before turning out and slicing.

THE THINGS I LOVE AND THE THINGS I HATE ABOUT FOOD

4 THE THINGS I LOVE AND THE THINGS I HATE ABOUT FOOD

When you are young your tastes are quite simple. You either love a certain food or ingredient or you hate it. Like Marmite. You learn that other mothers' cooking doesn't taste like your mother's, it's not really a question of better or worse to begin with, it's just different.

There's always the dread of going to someone's house and feeling you've got to be polite and eat something you loathe, or of there not being enough gravy, say, or bread sauce, or the custard being poured all over your pudding when custard makes you gag, particularly packet mix with a wrinkle of skin congealing on top. A boyfriend's mother did that once, flooding my helping of apple pie, and to this day I have no idea how I neutralised my taste buds and my choke reflex: it must have been love.

Then there's the food you've never tried before, or a dish that looks like one thing but turns out to be another. I remember the first time I dolloped mayonnaise on at some elderly friends' of my parents and it turned out to be that claggy, vinegary, bottled apology, salad cream. It permeated the salmon, I couldn't scrape it off, I'd been taught to eat everything on my plate: there was nowhere to hide it. The day was destroyed, my palate was nuked. It coats your teeth like enamel and malingers like rancid garlic so that you go on tasting it for hours even if you try to neutralise it with something stronger: Trebor mints, espresso, blue cheese.

Another time I greedily heaped spoonfuls of crisp roast potatoes onto my plate only to find that they weren't potatoes, they were parsnips. I love parsnips now, but their sticky sweetness and yielding texture were revolting and shocking and I was expecting something else. Akin to the dining club at Cambridge whose annual drinks party in one of the Fellow's gardens one year consisted of handing out cornets stuffed with chocolate ice cream with the wine. I licked, my mouth stammered in alarm, I bit and lobbed the strange substance around my mouth. It was chicken liver pâté.

You begin to develop fads, often when you're a teenager: food is the one form of control you can exercise, if only in a small way, over your otherwise heavily arm-guarded world in which parents, teachers, your friends' parents, your grandparents – all the grown-ups you know – have their say in what's best for you. They tell you to eat up what's on your plate, that you can't have pudding until you've finished your greens, they bribe you with treats: chocolate, sweets, the promised elixir of your favourite cake or ice cream, but you've got to be good. Very, very good, to be allowed to indulge in what you're then told for the rest of your life is bad for you. Whoever bribed a child with broccoli or rhubarb? But why not?

Even writing this, it is obvious how we use food manipulatively, utilising our personal understanding of portion size, control, nutritional know-how, our desire to nurture, by nurturing those we love with food selectively and calculatingly. There is no other area of a mother's life where she has more control over her family than food. And every mother's behaviour is predicated on prejudice, childhood experience, body image, peer group, supermarket, medical and food industry pressure, personal taste.

How crazy and ill-informed is the current obsession with food allergies; our vetoing animal fats and protein, red meat and cheese, eggs and cream on scant understanding of our body's needs. We deprive ourselves of what we want so all we can do is think about it, like an addiction, until we then eat too much of it because that's what deprivation does.

Better not to give it up in the first place. A fast, or famine, leads to a feast.

Is it polite to serve organ meats like liver, kidneys, sweetbreads or brains without asking your guests first whether they have a horror of innards? To dish up a raging vindaloo or even a mild Moghlai without doing a spice test of your friends first? To not ask if there's anything they can't eat before you invite?

Conversely, is it rude to say to your host 'I don't touch dairy or red meat or wheat' when you are invited to lunch?

I think it's exceptionally rude but others think it's polite, or at least reasonable, as it's in their own interests. I mean, I think it's rude to give a list. If you're a vegetarian, please speak out, but do I really have to note all your most un-favourite ingredients if I ask you to dinner?

And so to quantity.

I remember a neurotic New York lady looking positively frightened when I served her a three-egg omelette as 'baveuse' as a Frenchman would weep for. Not at the runny aspect, surprisingly; she had asked me to make her an omelette because she didn't know how to cook this simplest of dishes, and then feigned horror at the size of what, to we normal mortals would have seemed, well, normal. At home, she told me, she ate only egg-white omelettes. A bit like eating a steak tartare without the steak.

'An egg-white omelette is not an omelette,' I wanted to shout. But she wouldn't have got the point.

And what, exactly, should one do when faced with food so bad that even one's well-drilled manners go into meltdown? It's all very well dining out on the story afterwards, but here are a few that give pause to the thought that one should, at all times, eat what's on one's plate and tell the hostess it was delicious.

I have been served still frozen in the middle Aunt Bessie's roast potatoes by an otherwise brilliant hostess whose company and the company she kept – all ages, all stages, all backgrounds, politics, persuasions, religions, intellects in the mix – was brilliant and sparkling, but who was proud of her no-cooking skills and thought food, like sex, should be endured rather than discussed and was beneath consideration, the province of inferior minds. Her pièce de résistance pudding-wise was melting a block of that cheap, pig-fatty bright white ice cream, stirring in a little blackcurrant purée and refreezing it. Or serving a block of Vienetta to save time.

Then there was the soup my daughter Charissa and I couldn't fathom a single ingredient of at supper with a notoriously uninterested and arrogant-in-the-face-of-ignorance cook. We moved on to her pride and joy, réchauffé mashed potato that was starchy and rancid from sitting fridge-bound and had a sort of vinegary after-taste to it. But the soup, its tawny brown sludgy depths indefinable and murky, what could it have been, how could anyone achieve such disgustingness? What could we call it? 'Chutney soup,' Charissa insisted as we cried with laughter all the way home.

Then there was a mean, penny-pinching hostess who proudly showed off her economical country ways by inviting everyone she knew to a party and 'clearing out the deep freeze' of last year's game. Some of the birds were a tough, dank, yellowy green so the sobriquet 'last year's' was a blatant lie, and the 'cassoulet' was interpenetrated with tinned kidney and flageolet beans, about which she said, with a dazzlingly convinced pride at her clever austerity and trickery, 'I never use a recipe.'

The friends who have known me from back in the day never try to impress. They know what I like when I go to dinner with them, and they cook how and what they love to cook. Be it oxtail or liver and bacon, roast beef or La Bouillabaisse, who would prefer the hostess in a fluster, trying to impress, to the hostess comfortable with a dish she loves to cook, however simple, and feels she has got to the essence of?

I loved a recent offer from a man who had never cooked for me before but who was clearly unfazed and enjoying the contemplation thereof: 'I may cook for you or I may take you out to dinner as my oven's up the swanny. Not that I'm frightened of cooking for you.'

My riposte: 'Nothing like a heat-and-eat dinner.'

We went out.

Not because he felt the fear, but because he didn't feel like stir-frying.

The worst threat I've ever had on the culinary front is from an old friend and food lover, Nick, who was my son's tutor at Eton and who has become, with his wife Sal, a dinner companion for life, the honours equivalent of being awarded a CH, or Companion of Honour.

'Have you heard of baboutie?' he asked menacingly some time ago, and I sort of knew that if I hadn't it was for a bloody good reason.

'Describe it.'

He is, by the way, South African by birth, but please don't take that as food racism.

'Well you cook the mince with curry powder and onion and raisins and then you make a custard to put on top of it and you add apricots...'

The look of terror and alarm must have registered deep in Nick's synapses. The dish has become a threat which I know, one day, he will carry out if just to see its full effect beyond the realms of my imagination.

Perhaps it could be a form of torture for prisoners or if you decided to have your worst enemies to dinner. I know I must never fall out with Nick or I may end up sitting in front of a plate of it. Short of tripe, which I've stomached but it hasn't stomached me, shiitake mushrooms, coined 'shit-ache' by my son Harry, milk – to drink or in rice pudding or junket – or green peppers, I can't think of a more unappealing concoction, one that would ensure I starved rather than ate, however starving.

Perhaps the greatest power food has is its mood-altering power.

If you are tired, angry, miserable, depressed, worried, nervous or any of the negatives we associate with an inability to feel pleasure, your senses change all that when you smell food and the current switches to positive once the plate is in front of you and you taste the first mouthful. The most primitive of instincts kick in: comfort, pleasure, fulfilment, satisfaction, and even after you have put your knife and fork down you are alive again and your senses have worked their magic. I have seen it even with the sick and dying; however briefly, no matter.

Come to think about it, it is this magic power that I love most about food, for when all else fails, food never does.

·················:··················

PRIMAVERA TART

Late spring and early summer give us the most magical triumvirate of vegetables: asparagus, peas and broad beans. You can add artichokes, baby turnips, carrots or pousse – young spinach – to the mix, but the first three make magic together.

This is a green tart. You can pack it fuller with tarragon, basil and parsley, or any of the three, you may add fried cubes of pancetta or a caul of prosciutto inside the baked-blind pastry crust, but I favour this naked greenness with a salt blast of Parmesan alone.

It is worth podding peas and double podding broad beans, I promise. Anything less would ruin its summer sweetness, greenness and taste.

6 fat stems of asparagus,
    or 9 more slender
    wands
450g peas, weight
    pre-podding
450g broad beans, weight
    pre-podding
1 dstsp each tarragon,
    basil and parsley,
    chopped fine
smidge of olive oil
300 ml carton double or
    Jersey cream
2 eggs + 2 yolks
sea salt and pepper
4 heaped tbsps Parmesan

makes a 24 cm/9 inch tart
serves 8

Preheat oven to 180°C/Gas 4. Chop the woody stems from the base of the asparagus, and throw into a pan of boiling water for 5 minutes, or until al dente when pierced with a knife.

Throw into a colander, and arrest the cooking process by pouring over cold water, dry them, then chop chunkily leaving the heads a little longer than the stems.

Pod the peas and broad beans. Throw the broad beans into a pan of boiling water and cook for 2 minutes, throw into the colander, pour over cold water, and double pod. Throw the peas into boiling water, cook for 3 minutes, drain, put in a bowl with the broad beans and herbs and add a smidge of olive oil to stop them wrinkling, toss.

Whisk the cream, eggs and seasoning together with the Parmesan. You may hold a tablespoon of the cheese back to add during the last 10 minutes' cooking, it forms a golden cheesy top to the tart.

Spread the peas and beans on the base of the tart, add the asparagus and pour over the cream and egg mixture.

Bake in the oven until risen and golden and just set, about 40 minutes. Remove from the oven and cool on a rack for at least 15 minutes before turning out.

This tart is delicious hot, warm or room temperature.

ASPARAGUS AND PARMESAN TART

Simple, bold, clear flavours, Parmesan and asparagus have always made excellent bedfellows, though this is not the classic dish where the Parmesan is shaved over the spears. In late April, May and much of June, when you can find English asparagus, this is your tart.

12 generous sized spears
  of asparagus
90g Parmesan
200 ml double cream
2 eggs + 2 yolks
sea salt and pepper

makes 24 cm/9½ inch tart
serves 8

Preheat oven to 180°C/Gas 4. Bake the shortcrust pastry in the usual way and dry it in the usual way (see p.196).

Cut the woody bases from the asparagus stems and plunge the spears into boiling water for 5 minutes or until al dente, it could be a little less, depending on the thickness of the stems. Cool, then chop half the spears, 6, into pieces, keeping the other 6 whole.

Grate the Parmesan and add it to the bowl with the cream and eggs and seasoning. Whisk together.

Place the chopped asparagus on the baked blind pastry as evenly as you can do quickly, then add the line of 6 in a row on top and pour over the custard.

Bake for 40 minutes or until bronzed and puffed up and just set.

You may add the last spoonful of Parmesan 10 minutes before the end of cooking time by just sliding the tart near enough to the oven door to sprinkle the top with the cheese.

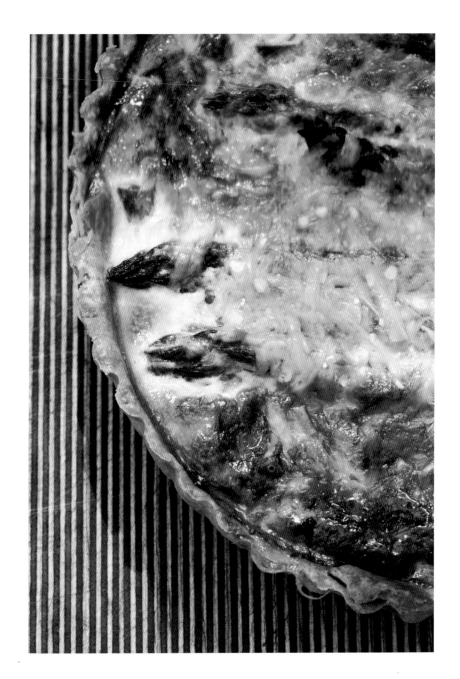

5 TREACLE TART

The best of tarts; the worst of tarts. Sometimes the toothacheing syrupy sweetness sends a shockwave that is almost, but not quite, unbearable. That is the thing about a sugar rush, you half love it, half hate it. You wish you hadn't. You don't know how to stop yourself. You do and you don't want to stop yourself, so the element of guilt adds to the pleasure, because you somehow think you should be more sweet resistant.

Treacle tart is another of those childhood puddings that lodges in the memory like the trunks in the attic, awaiting those moments when you return and open them, revisit them like old photographs, trying to remember who you were then, what you were thinking and feeling, what the occasion was. Your taste memory and visual memory might conjure up a near-as-damn-it accuracy, but the time and the occasion will always elude a little.

I remember walking illicitly from school, Bedales, to The Harrow Inn at Steep which has been an inconstant constancy throughout my life, and being less eager to drink the rough cider that befuddles after the first half pint – and in my case left me lying half buried in a beechy bank with a suitor once, for longer than it took to drink, on the walk back to school – than to eat their treacle tart with clotted cream. It was – still is – the deepest and most substantial of all the versions I've ever eaten. The middle is soft and almost fudgy with bread and the treacle clings to its depths in a gutsy, textured kind of way. The slices are double the size you would help yourself to if you were carving from your own tart, but I have never left a single, sticky crumb.

Then there was Mrs P's treacle tart. She was the wife of my grandparents' gardener Pollard. Mrs P came in on a Sunday to cook lunch and made the best roast potatoes, soused in dripping from the baron of beef until they were black and meaty; the best lemon meringue pie this side of paradise, and treacle tart, a very different one to The Harrow's. The filling was less deep, sharper, sublimely nutty with the malted grain from the bread, a gentler version which reflected the character of the cook. Mrs P was quietly spoken and a real Sussex countrywoman whose dab hand at pastry was all in her fingertips. The tart had a bevelled edge and twisted ropes of perfect, crisp pastry criss-crossed above the golden treacled filling. It was simple and as un-showy as she was; the crisp contrasting with the soft in the way that opposites attract, fatally and finally. It couldn't be a better marriage between the two.

My own treacle tart has metamorphosed over the years in the way that everything I cook has both technically and, I like to think, creatively. I can't play the same riff over and over without the need to improvise. What was a gelled middle because of the addition of a beaten egg and cream and the warmth from a pinch of ginger has now become sharper, nuttier, crunchier, less reliant on the lethal syrup. I add a coarsely grated Bramley apple and a clutch of chopped walnuts, more lemon zest from a sherbetty Amalfi lemon, more breadcrumbs from a nutty home-made wholewheat loaf.

My relationship with the green and gold tin is also about one of my great enduring friendships with a girl as golden as the syrup, Julia Roberts. This is, and always has been, something we share every time we meet, with what we call 'a glass of patience'. I will leave you to work that one out. If she is staying with me in Somerset or, as she was this summer, in Co. Mayo, the ritual is always accomplished. And then we buy her some green and gold tins to take home to America.

We are both girls of earthy, simple tastes. We heap on the clotted cream. We pour another glass, the beaded bubbles winking at the brim. I have never liked that old cliché 'glass half full'; think what you're missing.

We hit the Atlantic beaches with the children at full throttle, sustained by this tart of tarts. The children pour down the sand dunes in the blustery sunshine and we collect shells on the vast expanse of silvery, deserted strand to make boxes with. We lie in the surge and constant roar of the breakers rolling their length, with their cream crests breaking and sucking in the middle distance and Inis Turk and Clare Island beyond, the last landmass to abbreviate the horizon before America. It is the summer of 2012 and may only be 3.40 in the afternoon, and Julia says, 'Think we've forgotten to bring something. I sure could do with a glass of patience.'

TREACLE TART

*Adding the coarsely grated Bramley apple and the zest of 2 lemons stops the toothaching
sweetness that is almost too much to bear. You may add a large handful of walnuts too if
you want more crunch. If you don't have enough end bits of pastry to lattice the top it really
doesn't matter. A classic.*

450g golden syrup

3 tbsps double cream

2 small eggs

30g unsalted butter

zest of 2 lemons

**2 extra-thick slices malted
grain bread, crusts
removed, or
wholewheat bread,
blitzed to breadcrumbs**

**1 coarsely grated Bramley
apple**

**a large handful of walnuts,
optional**

makes 20 cm/8 inch tart
serves 8

Preheat oven to 180°C/Gas 4. Make shortcrust pastry,
bake blind in the usual way, dry out in the oven in the
usual way (see p.196).

Meanwhile, make the middle. Heat the golden syrup
over a gentle heat until it is thinner.

Whisk together the cream and eggs. Add to the
syrup, over a low heat, then add the butter in small bits,
the zest, breadcrumbs, grated apple and walnuts,
(if you're using them) and stir briefly to amalgamate.

Pour the panful over the base of the tart, add a
latticework of pastry strips if you feel like it, brush with
beaten egg-wash and return to the oven for 40 minutes.

Cool on a rack for 15 minutes before turning out and
serving. Clotted cream is equally as good as thin,
pouring cream.

SLOWLY

ELIZABETH DAVID

PatienceGray

Good Things   JANE GRIGSON

CLAUDIA RODEN

COOKED

6 SLOWLY COOKED

So what, exactly, is wrong with being a slow learner? With being not very good at all at something when you first begin. Of having no interest, no confidence, no particular desire to do it – marginally assuaged, in the case of cooking, particularly if you are a child, by the thought of eating what you have cooked – but getting there, what a waste of time, why bother?

Is it a pre-requisite of becoming accomplished at something that your talent shines through from Day One, that that talent is instantly recognisable by others?

This is teacher-lore, the way the educational system seems to work, the way the world and the world of work, works.

But read my brother Dan's early Drama reports from his prep school and it all flies out of the classroom window. I found a stash of them in one of my father's desk drawers recently after our mother had died and I had finally installed the circular, George II desk in its place, with the lithe, Franta Belsky naked nymph which Papa claimed was inspiration placed decoratively on top.

If the teacher in question were to re-read his discouragingly sharp, negative appraisals of the early, unschooled methods my brother was experimenting with, consciously or unconsciously, but with a kind of impulsion that eschewed wrong or unhelpful direction, well, he may just eat more than his words. Three Oscars later.

And what if you happen to be slow, yet good at something? Life is like one long exam, we have to get everything right first time, the end result has to be achieved speedily. It is as though we are applying the rules of competitive sport to the brain, but for no proven reason.

So, if you are slow...FOOD! Well, that's a subject for the unintellectual, the non-academics, the thick children who are good with their hands; send them off to be chefs, let the celebs amongst them write cookery books, recipes. Yet it matters not that they can't write, hate writing, for there is no place for real writing in cookery books. That was the thing of yesteryear when chefs stayed in the kitchen and authors who wrote about food wrote philosophically about food and its place in our lives. Writers such as M. F. K. Fisher, Patience Gray; scholar cook Jane Grigson; the joyous discoverer of the Mediterranean, Elizabeth David; scientist Harold McGee; Jeffrey Steingarten; food ethnographers and historians, Anna Del Conte and Claudia Roden.

These are writers who illuminated our world in the same way as writers of fiction:

novelists, poets, playwrights; who spoke to us of how food plays a seminal role in every experience we have from birth through life to death. How it can change our life, our love, the way we see the world, the way we think. Can make us understand ourselves better. Can fill our voids in body, mind and spirit, nourish the soul – just think about the lack of separation of those words, how holistic they are, how they define man and his relationships to the earth and his fellow man. Without food we cease to exist. Without good food, we cease to live. If we sideline its importance or its central place in our lives – the fuel element, eating to live rather than living to eat – we bear some responsibility for the consequences. Thus, in writing about food we are writing about life.

I didn't cook as a child. I had no interest. I loved to eat, I loved good food, but there were no signs that I would end up engaged in food at the level I am now, and no, absolutely no desire or inclination to do so. My career was as a film-maker, with writing a part of that.

When I was 13, alone at boarding school, remembering the comfort of Fortnum's blackcurrant ice cream, I tried to recreate it. I stirred Ribena from 'Pretty's', the school tuck shop, into double cream and added a little icing sugar and lemon juice. I have no idea how or what induced me or what quantities were involved, but I remember knocking on the kitchen window and handing the silver tray to the school chef and asking if he would freeze it for me. To my surprise he said yes.

And in that 'yes', my first unsupervised, original cooking experiment was born.

I went back, collected the frozen tray, deep, deep cerise pink, took it to my dormitory and chiselled out cold shards for my dorm mates. I knew nothing of how to churn or stir as the ice cream set to stop the ice from crystallising, but what we didn't know couldn't lessen the ultimate pleasure.

That, other than an omelette, was my soul experience of cooking for pleasure and making what I wanted to make until I left home for university. I knew no cooking techniques, had no cookery books, never, ever helped my mother in the kitchen if I could avoid it, and didn't do very well in school cookery classes. Baking was by rote and recipe. Ingredients were poor. White sugar, margarine, white flour, currants, glacé cherries, vanilla essence, Scotchoc, the sort of things I would run a mile from now. It was boring and repetitive and the only real pleasure I got then was from eating the end result, however burnt, rock hard, dry. Children are simply and only hungry. All the time.

So it took something quite major for me to see that maybe cooking was integral to life, mental and physical health, happiness, to find stimulus and satisfaction in the thought, the process, its accomplishment.

At 18, when my father died, my childhood ended abruptly. Going up to Cambridge, I think, looking back, meant I had to somehow re-establish the old order. Family. I had no family life. I had to create a new one. I had no skills, no idea how, but food, cooking, sitting around the table eating and talking with friends was my way back into the heart, the epicentre of life. Of finding my own people to love and nurture.

It has stayed that way, and it is possibly the most important philosophy I have passed on to my three children. I am not ashamed of that. I do not find food an inferior subject to think about, talk about, write about or indulge in.

When I am cooking, my whole creative and technical focus is on what I am doing. I am suspended from everyday life. Why that is equated with drudgery and choredom I know not, but it needn't be. It is a purpose and a pleasure in its own right if you decide to make it one. From my first utterly appalling attempts from the bibles of Jane Grigson and Elizabeth David, which I used cover to cover for those three university years and have referred to ever since, I realised I was onto something. Being self-taught may have been disadvantageous for those eating my food, but with the long view I can see that it was quite the reverse. It was like a method of enquiry you had to disseminate for yourself and constantly refine and alter alchemically, with both brain and instinct. The two come together in cooking as do all the senses. The learning is infinite and never slows. It is a fascinating craft. Repetition need never be dull as the fine adjustments keep it alive.

This was not a road I chose, it was a road that chose me. My film-making career was built on passion and the ambition to tell stories through film, a visual medium that relies on the word and the dramatic too, but where 'show, don't tell' is the dictum.

Showing is the best way of teaching people how to cook too, and without passion there is simply no point.

One of the great lessons I have learned is that we can surprise ourselves by simply having no idea how the road has led to what we are now doing. It has been imperceptible, it has backtracked, it has backfired. It has been frustrating, rewarding, difficult. I have always been a slow learner and a late developer, but I would argue that perfectionism is a part of that and that perfectionists can't help themselves, they do things at their own speed the only way they can.

When my son Harry was four, and in kindergarten, I found him shut in his bedroom with a pencil and a piece of paper writing out lines of each letter of the alphabet, painfully, slowly. I had no real idea why. His teacher told me he had refused to write them in class. Aha. He wouldn't show her his work until he saw that he could do it perfectly, how he wanted to do it. He was told he was slow at every turn. He refused to sing in public, in the school choir. He took three hours to do a maths prep that others knocked off in thirty minutes. Teachers banged on about how he would never be able to finish an exam.

At the beginning of his second year reading Biological Science at Oxford, when he told me that he had joined the renowned Oxford *a cappella* group Out of the Blue and I discovered that Harry had been practising singing secretly in the tiny gazebo at the end of the garden all summer before auditioning, I joined up the dots.

When I had been pregnant with him all those years ago, I went to hear Rosamund Plowright sing Mozart. Harry was doing whooshing great backflips inside me throughout. I remember sitting bolt upright in my seat thinking 'I've got a musical child.' Then wondering whether my instincts were crazy, but what else could I trust? Then, when he was a baby and I used to put him on his changing mat, something made me sing series of notes to him. His face would change attentively, his eyebrows rise like question marks, his eyes light up; he would sing them right back with perfect pitch and giggle with pleasure.

Nineteen years later he went from too-shy-to-sing to singing in public in front of huge audiences. He fronted the Oxford University Big Band. He is now setting out on the road to being a musician. He writes songs. He plays guitar and sings with his friend Luca in their band The Fireflies. Slowly, slowly.

················:·················

PEAR, HAZELNUT AND HONEY TART

Pears and hazelnuts are best in roughly the same season, October/November, but both are available all the year round and are happy and harmonious together, an unusual take on a Bakewell middle and every bit as delectable.

You need a honey of strong character as this is an additional note, and a very worth-while one, so runny chestnut if you can find it, it's really worth it.

If you are using ready-skinned hazelnuts, toast them a little first in a dry pan, until they begin to turn biscuit coloured and oily. You will then have a much more intensely flavoured tart.

Conference pears are best for cooking, they keep their firmness and flavour and don't exude too much liquid.

150g unsalted butter
2 heaped tbsps runny honey + 2 extra for when the tart is cooked
200g whole hazelnuts ground in the Magimix (if unskinned, toast in the oven for about 10 minutes then place on a tea towel and rub off the skins)
3 eggs + 1 yolk
60g vanilla caster sugar
5 large, preferably Conference pears
juice of a lemon

makes 26 cm/10 inch tart
serves 10

Preheat oven to 180°C/Gas 4. Make a shortcrust pastry in the usual way (see p.196) with 180g/90g flour to butter, and blind-bake and dry out. Meanwhile, make the middle: melt the butter with the honey, then pour it over the ground hazelnuts, eggs and sugar in a bowl and mix together.

Peel the pears, halve them, core them and dip them all over in lemon juice, allowing them to absorb as much as possible to prevent them from turning brown.

Place the pear halves in a concentric wheel around the tart base. Scrape over the hazelnut mixture, the little humps of pear will protrude.

Bake in the oven for 35–40 minutes or until the middle is set and browned and puffed up.

Place on a rack and cool for at least 25 minutes until warm before turning out.

Gently melt the extra 2 tbsps runny honey and brush it over the pears.

Serve with clotted or thick cream, this tart is best served warm.

APRICOT TATIN

The method below works for any tatin you wish to make, the classic apple, pear, pear and ginger or pear and blueberry, peach, plum, mango.

The apricot is so intense when cooked and doesn't collapse and lose its shape. Even its colour deepens, inside and out, and it looks a thing of beauty when you turn it out.

I have a special Le Creuset enamel tatin dish with handles on both sides. The crisp, caramelly tart turns out perfectly easily each time.

....

120g granulated sugar

2 tbsp cold water

30g unsalted butter cut into small pieces

24 apricots, split in half and stoned

1 sheet all butter puff pastry, fridge-cold

....

makes 24 cm/9½ inch tart

serves 8

Preheat oven to 190°C/Gas 5. Place the sugar on the base of the tin or enamel tatin dish evenly, add the water and cook over a medium to brisk heat, shaking occasionally but never stirring, if you do, the sugar will stick to the spoon. If a patch darkens prematurely, turn the dish and keep turning it so that the sugar browns as evenly as possible.

The moment the colour turns from golden to mahogany, remove from the heat and fling the little bits of butter all around the bubbling sugar.

Now press the cut fruit into the still erupting sugar.

When it has cooled down, roll out the puff pastry and tuck it like a bed-sheet all around the tatin dish.

Prick all over with a fork and brush with beaten egg.

Bake for about 40 minutes or until golden.

Remove to a rack for 10 minutes. Turn upside down onto a wide plate with a lip deep enough to contain the buttery, sugary juices. I think crème fraîche works best with this one, but please yourself.

Note: A right-way-up puff pastry apricot tart looks a picture of summer sunshine. I made this for my friends Grey and Neiti Gowrie in a trice, to consume on a beautiful day after we had eaten a giant crayfish. Roll out a sheet of all butter puff pastry to line (preferably) a 24 cm/9 1/2 inch square, greased tart tin with. Prick with a fork all over. Line up the 24 halved, stoned apricots like soldiers in rows, just overlapping a little then scatter on a little sugar, no more than a tablespoon all told. Brush the puff pastry edges with egg-wash. I allow them to overhang as a more relaxed feel is good for this tart. Bake at 200°C/Gas 6 for 40 minutes by which time the puff will be browned and shiny and the apricot edges will have attained that slight, black-edged pâtissier look. Cool on a rack and serve warm with clotted cream.

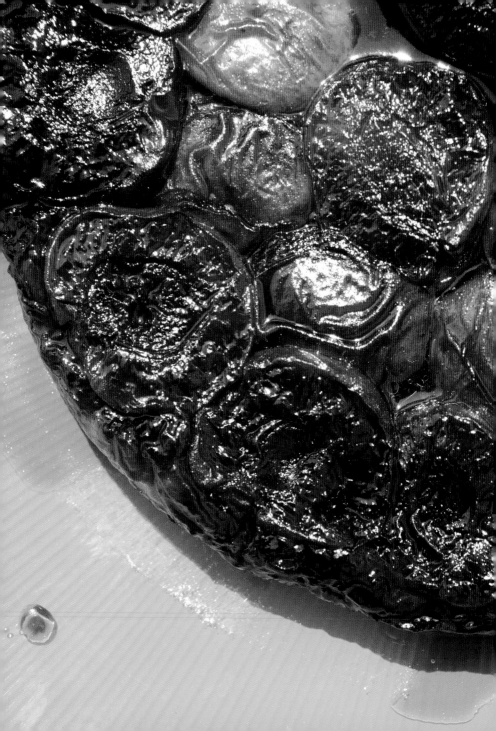

CHILDHOOD TARTS

7   CHILDHOOD TARTS

My three children have been reared on tarts. In fact, there was never a time during their childhood when they didn't beg for one or other of their favourites, or rail against the wholewheat crusted homity pies that I always baked the night before we set off for the Irish boat ferry every summer, knowing that their solidity and depth and substance would fill every hungry crevice on the journey and wouldn't crumble or smash in the meanwhile. Ballasted with cheesy mashed potato, thyme and a slice of tomato, each pie appeared to weigh in the hand almost as much as a small child.

The memories of the dishes my children hate have their place in our family's comic repertoire, in that they will never let me forget them. Last week when we were staying at our favourite hotel in Praz, below Courchevel, skiing, the children admitted they had almost taken the daily menu blackboard pinned outside and hijacked it so that they could write their version of the 'Suggestions du Jour' for me to find après-ski at the door, with the following: 'Croustade' and 'Boules de Semoule et Parmesan' – the last sounds hideous, but was, in fact, a divine Raymond Blanc recipe made with polenta and doused in a home-made tomato sauce. Somehow, it didn't make the cut. Unlike the tarts.

Luckily for me, walking in through the hotel entrance, I was, in fact, greeted once again with the subliminal, yet strategically placed sight on the sideboard in the hall of the tarts ready for the evening's dinner: Tarte aux Myrtilles aux Amandes, with its gooey seam of frangipane beneath the glossy bilberries, Tarte aux Poires, Tarte au Citron, Tarte aux Framboises, Tarte fine aux Pommes, Tarte aux Noix. How easily the French understand the importance of showcasing so casually what is at once expected and everyday, succorous to the soul, stimulating to eye, palate, appetite. A linear still life that looked as still and perfect as a painting, glazed with a painterly varnish and lined up for inspection.

When I wrote *The Art of the Tart* all of a baker's dozen years ago now, I really didn't see the consequences. I was following my passion and minding the gap. As in filling it: there were no other cookery books that I could find that exalted the savoury and the sweet in tart-form, so I decided to write what I couldn't buy in the hope that other people would want it as much as I did. I had no idea when I started writing what the different chapters would be about, but when the book began to write itself and I started cooking in earnest, certain themes emerged.

Other people's tarts gave me the opportunity of legally plagiarising tarts that I knew and loved from the great food writers and chefs and also from my friends who had tart stories to tell, some from their home countries, Sweden, Austria, France, Italy, Spain, others just with their personal best. There was a chapter on apple tarts because, really, they are a diverse story without end. There were the classics, there were the show-stoppers, there were those that I reconstructed from my own childhood memory, particularly a few from my west of Ireland summers like Butterscotch Tart and Canadian Pie. There were the American classics too, alongside my children's favourites that, in their turn, have mapped out their childhood memories.

Because I never made a song and dance about pastry as people seem, increasingly, to do now, saying they can't possibly make it for dinner, it is too time-consuming – two minutes from fridge to Magimix and back to fridge in my case, measured and timed – I can only believe that people see tarts as Tartes d'Occasion – my eldest daughter Miranda makes tarts with similar speed to mine and positively no fear of failure. Even when the baking blind of three lemon tarts she was making in a hurry the other day meant that the pastry shrank and fell from the tart sides and she had to start again, she did just that, ringing me in-between-whiles to ask what had gone wrong.

Heat too high, meltdown, you can't hurry with hotter, quicker.

It surprises her, that what was ordinary, everyday good food to our family, Quiche Lorraine, a Smoked Haddock and Watercress or Tomato and Oatmeal Tart – Jane Grigson declared it to be one of her only two or three truly original recipes which should give the rest of us pause for thought – is seen as somehow triumphant, feastly, special, to so many people she cooks tarts for if she is taking them to friends or doing a cooking job. Called to the bar she may be, but barristerial skills are no barrier to culinary ones and not seen as lesser in our family. And as for making a mistake, I fail to understand how that isn't seen as a positive when cooking. So many grown-ups say to me, 'Oh, I don't make pastry, I can't.' Recently I was accosted at the till in Waitrose by a lady behind me saying, 'Oh no, I know who you are, please don't look in my trolley,' which of course I immediately did, to see her ready-made pastry. 'I just can't make pastry,' she declared ashamedly.

Children are not frightened of getting things wrong, so what happens? Why, by the time we are grown-ups, do we give up when we don't get something right first time? Because we're brought up to believe that the worst thing we can do is make mistakes. Tell that to an artist, a writer, a musician, an actor, indeed, anyone in the arts professions. There wouldn't BE any artists of any sort if they believed that, they know that the only way of potentially doing something original is by doing it wrong, doing it again, maybe a little less wrong, and so on. I still get things wrong for heaven's sake and almost enjoy the post-mortem of working out quite why before a little subtle tweakery, of adding more or less of a flavour or ingredient. If cooking doesn't make you think, you're not doing it right.

So, back to *The Art of the Tart*, whose pictures I shot in my best girlfriend Janie's London house over far too few days for comfort. At times it felt like cement mixing, making pastry by the yard and timing six different tarts all with different fillings and crusts and at different temperatures with different cooking times. Miranda came as sous-chef, aged 15, to help cook the book for the camera. Any misunderstandings, anything unclear and she wrote belligerent notes in the margin telling me what she needed to know for me to edit. Miranda's initial cries of 'But I've never cooked this before,' were met, simply, with my saying, 'Well, the readers won't have done either, if you can get it right, so can they.' A risk, certainly, but a fair test to assume that anybody buying a tart book can make tarts if they can:

1. Read
2. Are prepared to make the effort
3. Have not just bought the book to drool over
4. Are intelligent enough when following instructions that say, like Miranda's once did to a friend, 'put the carrots in the bag in water and bring to the boil' not to do what her friend did: duly put the plastic bag filled with unpeeled, unwashed carrots into a saucepan and brought to the boil.

If I had to pick only one tart, my desert island tart, it would be my Tarte au Citron. Sherbetty, Amalfi lemons, rich Jersey cream, unrefined vanilla sugar, an almost shortbread-crisp sweet pastry, tartness that smacks the taste buds head-on and the slowest of cooking that gels the set to silkenness so that the primrose custard shudders as you lift each slice.

And the intensity of taste. It is like angels crying on your tongue.

Each of my three children have definite views on tart heaven.

Miranda is as sympathetic towards those who fear pastry as I am: 'People have just got to stop wittering on about their fear of making pastry and just get on with it and bake a tart. It is easier than driving to the supermarket, searching for the ready-made always hidden between the cheese and milk on the top shelf and getting it home to wrestle it out of its layers of packaging.'

Like all children delighting in their parents' shortcomings and peculiar peccadilloes, Miranda goes on to remind me of my 'Mrs Organic' phase when everything I cooked was brown:

I may have been taught to make a tart by the Queen of Tarts, but once upon a time, my mother used to make some of the worst pastry I have ever eaten. Her fillings were always a scrumptious, deliciously glorious marriage of flavours that redeemed her thick, dry pastry made with wholewheat flour. The slightly dodgy outer edge was left

uneaten, while we licked the last drops of whatever new chocolaty, fruity, sticky,
gooey, creamy, cheesy, syrupy, lemony, meringue-topped heart of the tart that we were
given the privilege of eating before anyone else.

Lucky for me, that I changed my ways and went back to the classic white formula and perfected my pastry skills. Otherwise I would probably only be allowed to tart-munch with daughter No. 1 in an approved, French patisserie.

Critical children are something I am proud of though, that's how I brought them up to see food, but if I'd got stuck in the hippy rut, who knows what we'd be eating now.

Every summer in July on Harry's birthday we have a weekend I look forward to all year. His old school and Oxford friends, now with girlfriends – wives even, some of them – descend and eat, sing, drink, swim along the coast at Porlock or Lynton, play croquet, have water fights in the garden, sing some more – the rule is, no serenades, no cooking on my part – and the sun shines in time for the sirloin of beef in the garden with a great table laid for anything up to two dozen for Sunday lunch.

And there are tarts. I had thought the classic strawberry with crème patisserie, those little French, sweet bonbons of 'Gariguettes' strawberries would be the favourite, but as Harry's text, when quizzed on the subject, insists:

This is The One: white choc and raspberry.
A better combo than the Owl and the Pussycat.
Hand-picked rasps from garden whose scent you can taste before you even bite.
Dark choc pastry one of the only pastry incarnations that's ever made me realise what
all the fuss is about, which along with the sharp acid kick of the berries stops the
sweetness getting out of hand. Evokes memories of all my favourite people being glut-
tonous, rowdy and cavorting round the garden with a hosepipe.

And in answer to my 'best tart' call, Charissa, my second daughter, a young actress, e-mailed the following:

Sorry, was in a rush to get to work this morning as even though I woke up really early
(5.30 a.m. for some reason) I was disorganised, even spent 20 minutes cutting a
pineapple, trying to recreate breakfast at Les Peupliers! I had a really nice recent
memory, when we'd just moved to Battersea, it was beautiful summer time, I even
remember what I was wearing it was so warm, and you'd booked The Only True
History of Lizzie Finn, by Sebastian Barry at Southwark Playhouse, and you had a
parking angel, and you brought up a hearty chunk of a slice of this delicious tart you'd
made, pastry, Parma ham, all the summer veg, asparagus, peas, broad beans etc,
some kind of cheese inside no doubt! We sat in the car eating a nice wodge of pastry,

then met that lovely old actor outside the back door of the theatre and he talked to us and let us in as we were unsure as to where the entrance was. His name was Andrew Jarvis I think and it was quite exciting to meet an actor before a performance. Harry met us there too and it was just a good, simple, summer evening, great play and good food memory attached. I liked when I was a child and it was just the 2 of us at home and you were trying to live off the garden and store cupboard and local farm eggs for a week and you made a herb tart from herbs picked in the garden. It truly was a dinner made out of nothing and it tasted yummy. Quiche Lorraine is a favourite for me just because I am a classic girl and yours tastes so good, plus you taught Gladys the recipe and she always made a yummy one for us too. I love smoked haddock and watercress tart and tomato and oatmeal tart too. OBVIOUSLY you make the best lemon tart in the kingdom.

'Memory attached,' as Charissa so succinctly describes. And with it, the distinctive voices of three children who I can only hope go out into life as unafraid to express themselves through their art and their cooking as they are with the openness and directness of their writing.

. . . . : . . . .

TARTE AU CITRON

To get that quakingly wobbly set of lemon custard that makes this the tart of tarts, the temperature of the oven has to be much lower for the second part of the cooking, and then you have to watch it like a hawk. Gently nudging the tin is the best way, and if only the very centre quakes, remove the tart, it will carry on cooking on the rack, hold your nerve.

Please make sure you taste the raw mixture, lemons come in all sizes, so you may need to add juice to get that lip-smacking tartness.

9 whole eggs
300g vanilla caster sugar
300 mls double cream
juice of 6–7 large lemons
and the zest of 3

makes 26 cm/11 inch tart, there may still be enough mixture for some smaller ones, depending on the depth of your tart tin.

serves 10–12

Preheat oven to 180°C/Gas 4. Make sweet crust or pâté sablée pastry (see p.198) with 180g flour, bake blind and dry out in the oven.

For the filling: in a large bowl, whisk the eggs and caster sugar together thoroughly. Pour in the cream and the juice of the lemons and taste, adjust accordingly. Think very tart, as there will be a slight diminution in tartness during the cooking process.

Add the zest, any earlier and it will get caught up annoyingly in the whisk. Scrape the mixture into a measuring jug as you can then pour it into the tart case which you don't need to remove from the oven.

Turn the oven down to 130°C/Gas 1. Begin to check after 25 minutes, but, depending on your oven and the depth of the tart, you may find the tart takes 40 minutes rather than 25 to set to a perfect, creamy, shuddery gel.

Remove to a rack and cool to room temperature.

Turn out and serve, or place in the fridge if you would like to eat it chilled, for a further hour.

Best eaten on the day, like most tarts, but particularly so with this. More cream would be too much of a good thing in my opinion, just place some raspberries turned in a little cassis or cherry or similar fruit eau de vie alongside.

SIMPLE APPLE TART

An apple tart is a lovely dish when you feel like a single decker rather than a pie.

8 crisp, good flavoured eating apples like Granny Smiths or Cox's

the juice of a lemon

60–90g vanilla caster sugar, depending on the sweetness of your tooth

300 ml best apricot jam to glaze with 1 tsp water

makes 26 cm/10 inch tart
serves 8–10

Preheat oven to 180°C/Gas 4. Make the pâté sucrée or sablée pastry (see p.198) and line the tart tin.
Prick with a fork and brush the tart with egg at this stage as it isn't going to be baked blind.

Peel, core and quarter the apples and sprinkle the slices with lemon juice before laying them in concentric circles from the outside in onto the uncooked pastry base.

Sprinkle the sugar over the surface and bake for 35–40 minutes. A cooked tart looks browned and cooked.

Warm the jam and water in a pan then brush it generously over the top of the tart.

Return to the oven for 5 minutes.

Cool until warm on a rack before turning out and serving with cream.

Equally good warm or cold.

WHITE CHOCOLATE AND RASPBERRY TART WITH A COCOA CRUST

Harry's favourite birthday tart. It reappears every July, but late raspberries in November mean you can still taste the fragrance of late summer, and the sharp, lactic crème fraîche offsets the terrifying sweetness of white chocolate and stops it being too sickly. I am writing this with four cocoa crusts just out of the oven, all made in one go in the Magimix, so this is something for a big party if you want special and easy. Make the filling first, as it needs to chill.

For the cocoa crust:
180g flour
2 heaped tsps Green & Black's organic cocoa powder
90g butter
2 tbsps unrefined icing sugar
1 egg yolk

For the filling:
200 ml crème fraîche
250 ml double cream
180g good white chocolate
400g fresh raspberries
a little cocoa powder to scatter

makes 28 cm/11 inch tart
serves 8

Heat the crème fraîche with 100 mls of the cream until just before it boils. Meanwhile, break the chocolate into a large bowl. Pour the cream mixture over the chocolate and leave for a minute before stirring until the chocolate has completely melted. Cover with cling film, poke a few holes in the cling film with a skewer to let the steam out and refrigerate for 2–3 hours.

Whisk the remaining cream until thick but soft, not rigid, and fold into the chilled chocolate mixture.

Preheat oven to 180°C/Gas 4. Sift the flour and cocoa powder into the Magimix, throw in the butter, sift in the icing sugar, add the egg yolk and pulse a few times.

Add 1–1½ tbsps chilled water and bring to a ball, flatten, cling film, chill in the normal way. Roll out and place in a 28 cm/11 inch tart tin.

Bake the pastry blind for 25 minutes. Remove the baking beans, prick with a fork, return to the oven and cook for a further 10–15 minutes, test for crispness by hand. This pastry you want completely cooked as this ends the cooking process. Remove to a rack and cool.

Put the raspberries in the cooled tart case and gently crush with a fork until they just begin to bleed. Pour the mixture over the top, smooth, and refrigerate for at least 2 hours. Turn the tart out cold and sprinkle with a tiny bit of cocoa powder.

homestart

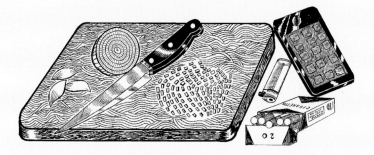

8 HOMESTART

I am not a natural teacher. I have always tended to side with the naughty child and I still do. And I haven't got the patience, I know I haven't. Aeons of boredom in the classroom meant I daydreamed my way through most of my schooldays, apart from the subjects I was interested in and good at, English, Art, French. If the teacher didn't inspire me, I lost interest, I didn't work. I couldn't write for the English teachers I found uninspiring. So they must have found the high marks I constantly got from my most inspiring teachers pretty unfathomable.

I have always wondered just how great the effect on exams – but really on life, a passion kindled – the very best teaching can have and thus consider myself extraordinarily lucky that I had three brilliant teachers, one at each of the primary, secondary and tertiary levels of my education, Miss Kemp, John Hetherington, Lisa Jardine. I would have done anything to impress any of them; I worked single-mindedly, obsessively focused; in all else I was lazy, dismissive, exclusory, chaotic in the way that, I suppose, passion drives everything else from view, it is a single-engined, single-minded beast. I couldn't contemplate a slip, however marginal, from the highest grade as it was them, the teachers who inspired me and their opinion that mattered most. I wrote for THEM.

I have always done my best work for my best editors, in both film-making and writing, and I acknowledge the immeasurable value their influence has had over my life and my career. They set the standard. They ensured that I at least understood how high their expectations were of me, thus mine of myself; how those expectations were not a static thing or open to negotiation, disbelief or disagreement on my part; they were continuously raised; no resting on lowly laurels.

The idea that pressure is a bad thing is simply foolish-minded. The best teachers know exactly what they want and what their pupils can give them. They start the debate within, of our being our own harshest critic and of learning that in life one has to do it for oneself, honestly, truthfully and with complete objectivity. Particularly in any of the arts where one is publicaly criticised. It's not just minding about a bad review – that is an acceptable indulgence, it's not humanly possible not to, and it's always the bad one we remember – it's about knowing the truth and the lie about it and learning to continuously rise above.

So what happens to the children who don't have any expectations of themselves because nobody else ever did, or because they didn't get around to finding out that they could achieve anything they wanted to if only someone made them believe they could?

I spent a few months last summer in a church hall in Minehead teaching a weekly cookery class to some young mothers who had asked their local branch of Homestart for help. The charity offers practical help and visits to families finding it tough rearing young children.

Somerset is a beautiful place to bring up children, idyllic in the obvious ways, but there is no beauty in rural poverty and isolation, joblessness, mental illness, drugs and drink. The city problems are, in a sense, compounded far from the madding crowd precisely because of loneliness, distance, low wages, and you have to have a car to get anywhere near civilisation. You can be marooned by the weather, live miles from anyone or anywhere, not get to meet other young mothers or fathers with the same stresses and strains on their hands, not want to look like you can't cope.

As I walked in through the door for the first time, I was the nervous one. I felt like it was my first day in a new school.

These girls didn't need another adult patronising them with matey-ness. They needed a break from their babies and toddlers who were being looked after in the church hall for two hours. They needed some fun. Someone to listen to THEM for a change, some time to do something for themselves, someone who didn't impose what they wanted to teach on unwilling ears and tell them what they ought to be cooking and eating. Look how badly wrong that went even for Jamie Oliver when he went into one school and changed the menus and the mothers were found poking hamburgers and chips through the railings at lunchtime to show they had the right to feed their children what they wanted to.

It's a fine line you tread telling anyone that you know better than they do, even finer if you start telling them what to do. So I kept the fact that I'd been told one of the mothers fed her toddler almost exclusively on a diet of ground up doner kebabs to myself and went in open minded. I got used, when I made my BBC2 series about the NSPCC, to finding children in houses with nothing but a deep fat fryer and a sack of spuds in the corner, or parents who hadn't given their children breakfast when the social workers arrived at midday, going to the fridge for the Mars bars. I had witnessed children removed from their beds and homes at night by the NSPCC officers from dodgy caravan sites where the only sign of food was the collar of lard welded rigid to the gas burner like set wax, a manky burnt frying pan the only weapon of culinary destruction visible. Judge not, and all that, but it is not my remit to impose my values on anyone nor for them to do the same to me.

I took a risk that first week. The budget was ludicrously tiny, £15, and for that, all four girls had to go home with supper for their families. I wanted to teach them about taste more than anything, how to make things taste good, but first I needed to know their taste. What did they like to eat and what could they cook? Were there things they wished they could afford to make or would really love to learn?

The first dish was going to be my calling card to either lure them the following week or ensure they didn't come back, so I had to really think it through.

I brought my children up on Puy lentil, pasta and tomato soup. More of a stew than a soup, it is thick with smoked bacon, herbs, Parmesan and the onion, garlic, celery and carrot soffrito to which the tomatoes and lentils are added give it strength and depth of flavour. It can be made in advance and heated up for days. A one-pot, basic skills peasant of a dish. Short of torching the pan, it can't go wrong whatever you do to it and the additions and subtractions you can make according to the fridge, your purse, your larder, make it something for all-comers. It is made with water, not stock, any cheap lentils will do if the Puy ones are too expensive, any herbs work, parsley, basil, tarragon, thyme, bay; you can forget the bacon if you're a veggie, so I thought this would be a dish which each girl could adapt to her individual taste. Making recipes by rote and rule might not work, if everyone could add their splash and dash of creativity, they might start to feel confident about cooking new dishes from scratch.

My worry about lentilphobia was entirely misplaced, as was my fear that it was not the sort of food they would want to try or thought their children would eat. Again, entirely misplaced, one girl said she often cooked lentils as they were so cheap and they were all eager to try something new. They hadn't cooked with fresh herbs before and one girl was vociferous about the Parmesan stinking of sick, but she was happy to grate Cheddar into the soup instead.

I demonstrated how to chop the vegetables for the soffrito. One girl had such poor knife skills she didn't know how to hold the knife and was terrified of it slipping and severing a finger. Another girl couldn't read, so we worked out a method of her watching me first and then between us we drew pictures of the quantity of each ingredient and she was amazingly quick and accurate at verbal instruction, it was a skill she'd developed in the absence of reading.

I have always believed that the eyes are the most important sense of the five for cooking, that things lodge better in the memory when you've seen for yourself. I discovered that kitchen equipment was pretty rudimentary in some of their kitchens, one girl had two small saucepans and a wooden spoon, but clearly loved cooking, was utterly absorbed by it, repeated the soup at the weekend at home with another of the girls and said they'd spent all weekend cooking together. Up till then, she said, she didn't really go out of the house as she had nowhere to go and didn't know any other young mothers as she was new to the area. One Monday she came in proudly saying that her dad had bought her a couple of new pans for her birthday.

In the absence of liquidisers and food processors I had to make sure all the dishes could be made by hand in the short time we had and that I taught the different processes from scratch the old-fashioned way.

At the end of our first session, everyone tried everyone else's soup. I think the girls' biggest surprise was that everyone's tasted different but they were all good. My final words that day were that if I had been given a bowl of their soups in a café I would have been thrilled, I would have returned, that they were all good, natural cooks.

It was clear that the smallest bit of praise initiated the biggest of breakthroughs. The following week, the girls all came back, and one of them had a cup of tea made for me within minutes of my arrival from that week on.

The fag breaks helped concentration, as did the fact that I didn't question them. I never remarked on the swearing. So it didn't feel like a classroom, it felt like a laboratory in which we were all doing the same experiment. Bit by bit I could ask if the girls would wait for the next ciggy until they'd completed the next process; they, in turn, began to ask me to watch their pans in their absence.

So, I asked, what do you really want to learn to cook over the next few weeks?

Tarts. Lemon meringue pie, quiche, treacle tart and Bakewell tart. They knew what the classics were alright.

Roast chicken and all the trimmings. One girl told me she wouldn't dare roast a chicken as she wouldn't know when it was cooked and she might poison her child.

Pasta sauces like meatballs in tomato sauce, lasagne.

Chicken curry, lamb curry, prawn curry.

Sponge cakes, scones and chocolate brownies.

Chicken risotto with the remains of the roast chicken, for which we made the stock first, and despite cries of 'It looks like dirty dishwater,' they wolfed down the result.

Beef stew and dumplings.

Apple and rhubarb crumbles.

Cheesecake.

And so, for the next couple of months, the girls came back each week and we tackled all of the above with only the best ingredients. Each girl learned how to make perfect pastry by hand. I only had to say the immortal words 'no soggy bottoms' for the mantra to enter the annals of the girls' oral culinary lexicons and be intoned every time we baked a tart 'blind' or they turned a tart out fresh from the oven and the tin.

It wasn't without incident. After an alleged theft, two newly firm friends became sworn enemies. I told them that the kitchen was a place of calm not a warzone and that if I couldn't trust them not to stab each other to death, I couldn't let them cook. There was a catfight outside during fag-break one Monday, but by the time the girls came back in, the threat of losing that evening's dinner was too much to continue the vendetta.

They loved it when I was under pressure. At the end of one session, I had to turn their cheesecakes out, still hot, in a hurry and was swearing at the heat of the tin as I wrestled with the metal and tried to stop the wobblingly set cheesecakes cracking or collapsing. One of the girls, I saw, when I looked up at them giggling, was filming the whole thing on her iPhone.

The kitchen had become a place where the girls could talk about their hopes, fears, problems, daily lives and cook without pressure or competitiveness. A couple of them said they looked forward to each class more than anything else they did all week. When the money looked like it had dried up, the girls said they would do a car boot sale and raise enough for us to keep going. The best thing was, they said they'd do it by baking cakes and selling them.

In the event, we managed to secure enough money to finish the term and all the dishes the girls had put on their list. Not one of them turned out anything less than delicious over the whole period.

The sad thing is, it had to end.

There was no more money.

My experience over those few months last summer confirmed my belief that it is in the kitchen that the real battle of education and confidence can be won through the achievement of culinary skills, but the sense of its being a shared endeavour is crucial. Over a shared recipe or chopping board, the unconfident cook can grow in stature and feel the pride that we all feel when we put a good, simple dinner on the table to nurture our family with; one that we have made simply, but with love and care, having taken that great step forward from knowledge to understanding.

I still miss the girls. I looked forward to Monday afternoons too: the excitement, the unpredictability, the camaraderie, the openness and willingness with which they accepted how I wanted to teach them because they knew it was all about them, and my belief that they could learn to share my passion if we all had fun.

...................:...................

QUICHE LORRAINE

This has to be the most maligned and bastardised of tarts, in the sense that so often people present a 'quiche' that bears NO resemblance to the peerless classic, and clearly have no idea what the classic involves.

The Quiche Lorraine is a top tart. When cooked by a top tart maker who understands it. Yes, it is simple, there are three key ingredients: cream, eggs and smoked bacon, so if they are not of the very best quality, your tart will not be, however good you might be at making tarts.

Streaky bacon is a must, you need the fat – I pour mine into the custard for flavour when I have frazzled it in the pan and snipped off the rind.

....

16 rashers best, smoked streaky bacon: 8 for the filling, 8 for on top
300 ml double cream, untreated Guernsey or Jersey if you can find it
150 ml single cream
2 eggs + 2 yolks
sea salt and white pepper

....

makes 20 cm/8 inch tart
serves 8

Preheat the oven to 180°C/Gas 4. Make the shortcrust pastry in the usual way (see p.196) and bake blind and dry out.

Meanwhile, make the custard: fry the first 8 rashers in a pan with no other fat or oil, and turn them regularly until they are well crisped and browned.

Remove the rashers from the pan, snip off the rind, and break the rashers into pieces.

Whisk the creams and eggs thoroughly with sea salt to taste and a good grind of white pepper. Pour the bacon fat into the bowl of cream and mix in.

Remove the tart case from the oven, lay the pieces of bacon on the base of the quiche and pour over the custard.

Bake until gloriously golden and risen and just set.

Cool for 15 minutes on a rack.

Meanwhile, fry the rest of the rashers and when you have turned the quiche out ready to eat, lay the strips of bacon over the top. A perfect and generous final touch.

LEMON MERINGUE PIE

A true classic, and one that all children seem to love as much as all adults, the sharp twang of lemon with the sweet, crisp, mallowy-middled meringue.

grated zest and juice of
   3 large lemons
45g cornflour
300 ml water
3 large egg yolks
90g vanilla caster sugar
60g unsalted butter cubed
   small
3–6 egg whites, it depends
   on how cloudy you like
   your meringue
90–120g vanilla caster
   sugar

makes 20 cm/8 inch tart
serves 6

Preheat the oven to 180°C/Gas 4. Make the usual shortcrust pastry (see p.196), bake blind and dry out in the oven.

Meanwhile, make the filling and the meringue: put the zest and juice in the top of a double boiler, and add the cornflour which you've whisked with 2 tbsps water first so that it is a smooth paste.

Bring the rest of the water to the boil and add it to the lemon mixture. Keep whisking over the heat until the mixture thickens considerably.

Remove from the heat and whisk in the egg yolks, sugar and butter.

Leave to cool while you make the meringue.

Whisk the egg whites to soft peak then scatter in a third of the sugar and whisk again until satiny and they don't slip out of the bowl when you turn the bowl upside down. Add the next third of sugar and whisk again. Test the stiffness in the same way. Best test ever invented in the kitchen.

Remove the tart from oven. Scrape over the lemon gloop. Scrape over the meringue, sprinkling the final third of sugar over the top.

Put the tart in the bottom of the oven and cook until the meringue has browned and when you tap the outside of it, it feels as crisp as snow.

Remove the tart from the oven and cool for 10 minutes before turning out and serving.

Single cream is best.

The Particular Spot

9 THE PARTICULAR SPOT

The place that I chose to paint in Glasgow is really just a little community – a little
back street where everyone knows everyone and the same thing seems to be the case in
the village where I live in the North-East.

I find that the more I know a place or the more I know a particular spot, the more
I find to paint. I very often find that I take my paints to a certain place, begin to paint
there, and perhaps by the end of the summer I have not moved from that place. In fact
I have worn a kind of mark in the ground – there is no grass left. I just leave my
paints there overnight and eventually a studio seems to have arrived outside. I might
just turn round in the middle of a painting and see something and run back and get
another canvas and do that, but it is still the same spot really, the same feeling that
I am trying to grasp.

Joan Eardley

The Scottish painter Joan Eardley who died 50 years ago at the age of 42, built an emotional relationship with places and with people, to the degree that she could paint them from the inside out, not the outside in.

In the Glasgow back-street tenements she befriended children, most notably the 12 brothers and sisters in the Samson family, through whom she portrayed the life of the place, its rawness and dereliction, their street-urchin rawness and character, with a humorous and unflinching eye that didn't confuse innocence with sentimentality.

She moved to Catterline, a small Scottish village and coastal harbour and lived and painted until her untimely death. She painted the rough with the smooth, majestic alongside microcosm. Big blasts of gale and lowering storms at sea and peaceful fishing nets draped and drying, hung gracefully in the breeze and representing the calm after the storm, the fisherman's return, human toil and the elements that define our relationship to nature. Nature's drama and its quietitude.

Eardley created bold, brave canvases and made sense and order of some of the chaotic, haphazard beauty in nature that takes place in even the simplest shape and form, the haystack, or, 'just the grasses and the corn – it's oats this year, barley it was last year. There's a wee, windblown tree, and that's all. But every day and every week it looks a bit different...'

It is easier to observe the minute changes in nature if you live in the country, but it's still about how you look.

I grew up with one of Eardley's haystacks. It was a constant through my childhood, hung in our dining room which was painted the slate grey-blue of an uncertain sea or sky.

I wouldn't say I stopped looking at it through familiarity, but it was a fixed point, and after a bit it became unchanging because I didn't change the way I looked at it.

A few months ago, I read that there was to be an exhibition of Eardley's work at The Scottish Gallery in Edinburgh and subsequently at The Portland Gallery in London, so I offered my haystack on loan. I was curious to see both how Eardley's work had stood up to time; how contemporaneous, or of its time it felt, and to see a complete range of her work in one space.

I went with my younger daughter Charissa. We were bowled over. The space and light had been calibrated as judiciously as the groupings of the work, and the size and scale of the exhibition likewise.

At so many exhibition openings I end up watching people appear not to look at the work. They meet, talk, drink and stand in the way of anyone who wants to meet, talk, drink and look.

Here, everyone was really looking and talking to their fellow observers, even the ones that happened to be standing next to them whom they didn't know, and talking about what they saw and what they thought, what they knew of the artist. There was an air of collective stimulation and awe, tinged with sadness. One felt the achievement, the A–Z, the arc of this cruelly short working life and its being cauterised mid-flow, yet the embrace of the collection showed us a kind of completeness, how deep and clear the insight was into the world she was portraying even in a haystack and thus, how we can all look at our world, within and without, if we choose to.

I asked Charissa how she felt about what she'd seen afterwards, and she said, 'Uplifted.'

So how much more do we see by venturing out beyond the confines of Eardley's 'same spot'. Well, naturally it depends how we look and where we look; for how long we look and what stage of life we are at. In the rush for experience, new experience, the thrill of exploring a new place, a different way of life, we start to make comparisons and weed out the temporal from the enduring. The new place or experience does, though, re-connect us with home and a stronger, deeper attachment to it which we sense each time we return. But the constant search for paradise? For a place on earth that is almost pre-lapsarian in its innocence and beauty and perfectly temporal climate. Where sunny blue sky meets sparkling blue water via a golden ribbon of sand.

It is not Joan Eardley's world and it is certainly not mine.

There are places which have the same effect on me as Eardley's makeshift outdoor studios, where, the better she got to know her immediate surroundings, the more she found to paint.

One is the headland walk that I take from my cottage in Co. Mayo in all weathers and all seasons with my children and anyone who comes to stay.

Another is the more domestic setting of the kitchens and tables that have been fixed points in my working and cooking life; which, like Eardley's studio, change seasonally with the people, the light, the temperature, the scents and sounds of the dinners and conversations that fill them. And with the accumulation of time.

Cooking, like music, painting, dancing, words, life, the seasons, is all about rhythm. That same feeling that Eardley is trying to grasp, each time she paints, is really no different to what I try to create on the page or the plate.

I have been writing this chapter seated at the circular, Victorian dining table that once graced the dining room at the houses I grew up in, first in Kensington and then in Greenwich. The table from which, as we ate, the picture of the haystack hung alone on an adjacent wall. The table came back into my adult life quite recently and is now in the kitchen in the little house in Battersea that Charissa lives in and I part live in. The split down the middle of it is where my father, prone to infrequent and short rages which were over without consequence or retribution like a spring rainstorm, slammed his hand down and cracked right through the wood. There is also a burn mark from where one of my godmother's husbands tried to show off a magic trick with a tower of match sticks built like a miniature scaffolding which he then lit, but if the skill was to not set fire to its surroundings, it didn't work.

The kitchen table that has been the centre of my three children's lives as they grew up in Somerset is also a fixed point although it moved with me after my divorce to a new home. It became, at that point, the anchor that pulled us back to gravity as a family despite the new house being a house before it gradually settled into being a home. The table just started to write a new history, a new story. Around its rectangular pine top, scrubbed bone white, my three children have eaten their breakfasts, lunches, teas and dinners, debated, quarrelled, done their homework, played games, mixed laughter with tears, celebrations with drawing, painting, music, and eaten their early attempts at baking and cooking with friends and family.

Etched into the wood, those childhood memories run river-deep, the table a symbol of much that has built them as people, with the tangible, yet invisible comfort that just sitting down at its known, well-loved, homely surface imparts.

In my dining room, I have the long, narrow, shiny English 18th-century oak refectory table that once belonged to my grandparents, so continuity from the generations of my family has been preserved through food, wood, and the ceremony of sitting down to a properly laid table. It has more of a feeling of formality, is where we eat when we are too many for the kitchen table and for birthdays and parties, so the table has become associated with life's great, festive events and with the favourite family dishes that are served at it.

I have written books and articles, stories and essays, letters and memoirs at all these tables, including the kitchen table in Co. Mayo where I have spent over 20 summers. I have written synopses for the documentary films I made for 20 years and entertained cast and crew and editors as we play our parts in the slowly unfolding drama of the film we are making and the lives we are leading. One creative life has elided into the other, the directing and producing and writing films with the food writing and cooking. But it has always been at the table that creative decisions have been tossed and turned and batted around until consensus of a sort has been reached, only to change the following day on the road filming or in the cutting room.

And so to the headland. The place where one world meets another; where a great landmass meets the Atlantic Ocean, whose primitive, edge of the world feeling is augmented by the unpredictable and violent storms that scour the surfaces of its sea, the sky and the land. It is a primitive landscape and has its own, unique elemental energy that you cannot fail to feel just by gazing upon it; it is not for those who like a tamer version of nature. The sparse few trees are whipped and bent double by the winds and never grow to any height. The bog behind the house changes from its summer colours to russety brown in autumn, patched with lime bright bog mosses and silky soft stalks of bog cotton. The granite mountain, Mweelrea, lords its presence over all around, even the sea, and on the few days it is safe to climb, I never linger on its summit, for the cloud scuds mercilessly and secretly towards it and can hang over its peak for weeks. That would have one falling to certain death, as the summit is sheer for 350 degrees of its circumference and you cannot see the torturous way down if the cloud mantles it.

Walking down the snake of track from house to beach you can be blown sideways or backwards, almost picked up in a gust. The beach that leads to the sea is approached through sharp-grassed dunes and then you walk up through a narrow, sandy pass onto the headland itself, the grass cropped like a crew-cut by the sheep which graze the commonage. The sea is to your left, along with Killary Bay, Ireland's only fjord, the mouth of which you can see from the base of Mweelrea. Beyond, on Killary's south side is the rise and fall of the lavender blue Twelve Bens, a low range of mountains that switchback through the wilds of Connemara and which serious climbers can climb in a day, cloud permitting.

As the headland stretches towards the open sea, there are great chunks of ancient boulder bedded into the land that look as though some catastrophic event has hurled them towards the sea from an unseen height. One giant rock looks like the head of a prehistoric creature. Ahead are the islands of Inis Bofin, Inis Turk and to the right, the sugar lump shape of Clare Island.

This August when we followed the edge of the land, jumping down through the rocky approaches to the small bays on our way to Thallabawn, we came round a promontory and found dolphins arcing in unison as they came close to the shore after the shoals of mackerel. If we are on the boat, we have known heavenly moments when they have suddenly appeared from the deep to swim alongside us so close we could almost stroke their shiny, wet bodies, playing, chasing, begging us to join in.

There is a point at which you climb the last bit of green headland thinking that there is only open sea ahead, and then the most magical sight appears to the right like a mirage. It never fails to fill me with joy. Thallabawn. An empty, silver strand frilled with dunes, splattered with shells, the waves tumbling and sucking, drawing and pulling along its mile-long length to the tidal river that flows into it at its furthest edge. If it's a full moon and the tide is high, we have to wade through the river shoulder deep to reach land and road again. On a low-tide day we still have to stumble across its seaweedy rocks to the shore and up the road home, its narrow, twisty uphill path flanked by bushes of dripping crimson fuschia, flame coloured montbretia and purple loosestrife. Had Eardley set her easel down here she would never have moved.

The two hours it takes to walk the headland – longer if you tumble into the waves and then run the beach to the river to keep warm – are never the same.

People have asked me over the years why I don't go somewhere new as though I have limited my vision and experience, but this is the place that pulls me like the magnetic mountain, back to it. Like the summer swallows, I almost smell it come June and begin to yearn to fly home. The light is always moving and always moves, the skies and the sea are a meditation even when they are in uproar; you can feel your soul restored, the beat of the waves and their distant roar a constant, you regain something of what you have lost over the year each time, it is a replenishing, which drip-feeds into you little by little, almost, but not quite imperceptibly. It penetrates like a deep happiness and it would be greedy to ask for more or different, you are almost passive in the process if you are open to it. How many places can you say that about? Why would you trade the known for the unknown, the discovered for the undiscovered? You discover here, how few your real needs really are and that is enough in itself.

Sometimes we picnic in the spit of green lawn in front of the cottage and see the complete headland like a picture before us, bar the hidden secret of Thallabawn. Sometimes we take a rucksack and have lunch in the dunes, a tortilla, a tart, home-made bread, great wedges of lemon or carrot or ginger cake, tomato salad.

If you try to make sense of the world or your place in it, you are unlikely to do so purely by conscious thought. You learn that there are places where the questions you are asking, the dilemmas that face you, the decisions that you are not quite able to take, diminish in size because the hugeness of this landscape gives you another sense of scale and value and importance. From this emptiness, emptying the mind, the empty landscape, its powerful presence, things sort themselves out a bit. I am not being hopelessly over-romantic and unrealistic here and saying all problems vanish under a west of Ireland sky, but what I am saying is that small miracles do happen. A place can restore creativity, strength, mental and physical health, perspective, mend a broken heart, get a problem that seemed insuperable into a manageable shape and size. And just looking will give back to you what Eardley describes, 'the same feeling that I am trying to grasp', each time.

...............:................

SCARMORZA, FENNEL AND TOMATO TART WITH MUSTARD GRUYÈRE

This is a completely self-contained and perfect picnic tart to be eaten warm or at room temperature. Scarmorza is a delicately smoked fresh mozzarella, if you can't find it, use mozzarella di bufala. The filling is only cooked for a brief time, which means the mozzarella holds its shape and doesn't go stringy.

3 fennel bulbs cut and caramelised (as per the Crab and Fennel Tart recipe, see p.124)

1 tbsp Dijon mustard

4 tbsps grated Gruyère

8–10 large tomatoes, sliced

450g scarmorza or fresh buffalo mozzarella

3 tbsps best olive oil into which you have snipped any or all of the following:

1 tbsp chives, basil, parsley, tarragon, summer savory

makes 28 cm/11 inch tart

serves 10

Preheat the oven to 180°C/Gas 4. Make shortcrust pastry (see p.196) with 180g/90g flour to butter ratio, bake blind and dry out in the usual way.

Bake the pastry blind then return it to the oven and almost complete the baking, 10–15 minutes, touch to test it is crisp and biscuit coloured.

Remove from the oven and spread the mustard over the hot pastry base then scatter over the Gruyère.

Arrange alternate slices of tomato and scarmorza or mozzarella in concentric circles, then brush with ⅔ of the herbal oil.

Return to the oven for 10 minutes.

Remove from the oven and brush over the rest of the herby oil.

Cool until warm on a rack. Scatter over the Gruyère and slices of caramelised fennel.

CRAB AND CARAMELISED FENNEL TART

This could be the best crab tart I've ever invented. Fact. Not arrogance.

The caramelised fennel gives the rich, brown and white meat a sweet astringence and texture and crab being one of the few crustacea that it isn't sacrilege to add cheese to, the Parmesan, mustard and cayenne give body, strength, salt, a breath of heat. Warm is best.

400g crabmeat, equal white and brown
1 tbsp olive oil
3 fennel bulbs
2 dstspns unrefined granulated sugar
sea salt and white pepper
300 ml double cream
2 eggs + 2 yolks
a knife-tip of cayenne
1½ dstspns Dijon mustard
2 heaped tbsps Parmesan, grated

makes 24 cm/9½ inch tart
serves 8

Preheat the oven to 180°C/Gas 4. Make the shortcrust pastry in the usual way (see p.196), bake blind and dry out.

Meanwhile, make the middle: scrape the crabmeat into a large bowl. Heat the olive oil in a heavy-bottomed frying pan. Remove the tough outer leaves of the fennel bulbs, halve each, and slice vertically down so that each half is in three and doesn't break up because it retains some core.

When the oil is hot, scatter over the sugar and press the 12 pieces of fennel down into the sugar. Season.

Sauté at a brisk heat, turning when each side has caramelised to a beautiful bronze. Once the central core is barely resistant and the main bulb softened, remove from the heat.

Add the cream, eggs, cayenne, seasoning, mustard and Parmesan to the crabmeat and whisk to amalgamate.

Place the pieces of fennel over the pastry base. Scrape over the crab custard and return to the oven for 35–40 minutes until tremblingly set and bronzed and puffed up.

You may keep a tablespoon of Parmesan to scatter over the tart for the last 10 minutes' baking if you feel like a crusty golden circle atop the tart.

Remove from the oven to a rack and cool for at least 15 minutes before serving.

A salad of cucumber or broad beans, or a tomato salad with a mustard dressing are both great accompaniments.

10 **REVOLUTION**

S omething happened in the '6os that may, at the time, have appeared to have nothing to do with everything else that was happening in the '6os, yet, looking back, I am stunned that I have only just made the connection.

In the midst of the sexual revolution, which held sexual liberation as its founding principle, was a more discrete, less moral-eclipsing revolution: a food revolution. More of which later.

Unmarried mothers, divorced women, abortions, almost foolproof contraception, career women; as the movement gathered momentum, propelled by the pill and its promise of sex without consequence, there was a seismically swift shift from the old morals to the new. The collective hearts of the post-war generation of women were wooed and won by this apparent freedom and men, certainly, weren't going to object. Their responsibility became largely ours. The nature of womanhood was changed forever in an evolutionary blink.

Except it wasn't. For those of us just entering adolescence and womanhood in the '7os, we took the whole thing for granted, it was simply new to us in so far as it was part of the process of growing up, we'd never known anything different. We learned the rules from our peer group not our mothers, with whom the whole idea of discussing our sex lives was alien; parent/child formality saw to that. Something else that has changed completely between our generation of women and our children.

In fact, the revolution became as driven by the new culture of saying what you felt and how you saw things and shocking the previous generation's tenets, as it became known for its eschewing the old principles and way of life. This was not a quiet revolution, it was an articulate, outspoken one. But what we could now do practically, in the form of contraception, we didn't really understand the impact of; how giving us this extraordinary choice, these new rights over our bodies and hence our minds, actually took away our choice, our ability to choose carefully, sensibly, with due diligence. We had the option of seeing if we could behave and feel and think like men. That was probably the most damaging thing of all.

We didn't understand the implications of all this properly until years later. In a way, we surrendered everything to the notion of our freedom. It's a bit like coming out of jail after a long sentence and not being connected to the world you left behind, not belonging anywhere, yet eager, hungry for all the experience you've been denied, thus making up for lost time. But without a period of readjustment and reflection it cannot work.

When a generation wins a battle that has been being fought for generations, there is always going to be fall-out. We saw the changes we wanted and were entitled to as women, and the science helped provide them, but we couldn't see the short- or long-term effect of these changes either on ourselves or on the rest of society: men.

I think the impact has been every bit as great on men as it has on women and – this may be a highly contentious thing to think – I think men and manhood and relations between the sexes have gone through a protracted period of disharmony, conflict, lack of mutual understanding and trust, and rearrangement as a result. They needed to, pendulums always swing too far, but it's been a tough transition.

I am not saying this is a bad thing, but from personal observance, the sexes went head to head in battle to reconcile age-old differences that had probably been simmering with quiet, understated fury under a veneer of civilised behaviour for many, many years. Men had to understand that we had options and that it wasn't always about them. And that we weren't merely domesticated goddesses, chattels, the weaker, fairer sex.

And so the three-meals-a-day, perfect housewife left her unpaid job of domestic drudgery and went out to work. And to the supermarket. And to the ready-made, heat-and-eat meal. And many women began to sneer at their peer group if they were stay-at-home, make-and-bake mothers keeping the old traditional roles alive and bringing their children back from school to a home-cooked tea, then pouring their husband a drink on his return from work and cooking his dinner. We deprived ourselves of the choice we had fought for by making mothers who wanted to keep their traditional role inside the family feel like second-class women. The sisterhood turned on its own, to some extent, women didn't dare say they didn't have a job to other women, 'What do you do?' became more important than finding out who you were. And women bosses, struggling to prove their credentials, in the dog-eat-bitch world of office politics, had to be twice as good and committed to succeed. In their quest for the top, they behaved badly towards other women they were in competition with, whilst the men sat tight with their old-boy networks and prejudices.

This may be part generalisation, but it is not over-simplification; there are exceptions, but in the cut-jugular world of television that I was in, the all-male hierarchies kept women well below the professional peaks of the industry to a large extent, as they did in the medical profession. The management and the boardroom, senior editors and executive producers were 'suits'. With no more than a token skirt.

I had been accepted in the first batch of women by King's College Cambridge. I had been at England's first co-educational boarding school, Bedales. I had never had to question equality or women's rights, indeed, like Ireland's first female president, the brilliant Mary Robinson, I didn't believe in women's rights, I believed in equal rights. When I went to Anglia Television I discovered a bastion of male superiority. There were no researchers, producers, camerawomen or editors, programme controllers or board members of the female sex bar one lady director. The girls who I first went to work with sat behind typewriters and were PAs to the directors. I became the first female researcher there a year after I arrived, and was accepted by the ACTT shop on applying for my union ticket or I wouldn't have been confirmed in my position. The head of personnel had serious misgivings about my being given the job, largely because she wasn't sure whether my clothes represented the company image – leather trousers, a wolf-skin coat. On the other hand, the camera crews and editors had voted me unanimously in. They were all male. It may have been the trousers!

My first two bosses were male and made it quite clear what their empires were all about. One told me he hadn't employed me for my writing talent, but as part of his 'stable'. He would take his favourite girls out to lunch and keep the likes of me working till as late as he could on a Friday night when he knew I had the long drive back to London. The next boss, when I became a researcher, made absolutely sure that the tasks he gave me were almost impossible to accomplish, as though he were sorting out the girls from the men. He was rude, abrasive, dismissive, chippy and criticised everything I did, however well or efficiently, as though I should have to pay for the position I had arrived in in blood. He had clearly never dealt with an intellectual equal of the female sex before, particularly one with rather better academic qualifications than his own.

The men didn't want us heading up the TV totem pole towards their jobs.

They didn't want us behaving towards them how Mrs Thatcher went on to behave towards her cabinet.

They didn't know any better than we did quite how to replace the old order or with what.

A few years before I entered this world, I had taken my first steps towards culinary independent thinking even though I couldn't cook.

At 17, I was going out with a man twice my age. He took me to my first grown-up dinner in an Italian restaurant in Soho, and opened my eyes to a world I had never encountered. It was the dawn of the age of Aquarius, the musical *Hair*, hippies, and the germination of the brown-rice-and-sandals peace and love brigade. There was a move against post-war austerity and its diet of meat and two veg.

Vegetarianism was in its infancy and considered weird and 'alternative'. Wholemeal pastry, pulses, the Doris Grant loaf – wholewheat, no knead – no need to – seeds, salads, and earthy, rainbow coloured foods based on vegetables, fresh herbs and spices gradually became a part of the new-wave culture that sprouted in the '60s and took root in the '70s.

My first stand was to become a vegetarian at school, where the meat consisted of gristly stewing beef, shocking pink spam fritters encased in greasy thick batter, tinned corn beef hash, grey roasts. I was frowned upon with undisguised contempt by my peers. At that stage when teenagers need to conform with each other to achieve cool, I had gone markedly off-pitch.

It got worse when I started carrying around a rucksack which I filled with nuts, seeds, granola, live yoghurt, bottled organic celery and bilious-looking beetroot juice.

At home for the holidays, my mother refused point-blank to allow my new food-lore to enter her kitchen and to have any truck with my budding principles and vegetarianism. My first attempt at having any control of my life was rebuffed and ridiculed, but I still hung onto the notion that the whiter-than-white of the bread, pasta, rice, sugar, cakes, buns, biscuits and the plethora of industrial, processed foods like margarine and golden syrup weren't good for mind, body, soul or bowels.

And then I discovered that it wasn't just weird loony hippies who had gone down this culinary route.

Cranks Restaurant first opened its doors at the beginning of the '60s well before it registered on my radar, setting up shop midst the hub of '60s boutiques in Carnaby Street, the coolest street in London. In the late '60s, it moved round the corner to Marshall Street, which is where I first saw its daily queue snaking down the street and around the corner. I joined it. I didn't know it at the time – I didn't become a regular until the mid-'70s – but the founding principles of Cranks incorporated all the elements of the burgeoning culture and change that were beginning to rise like yeast to the top of society and permeate it at all levels.

The owners of Cranks loved craftsmanship – the founder was a designer, interested in sculpture, pottery and painting, and all the plates and mugs in the restaurant were made of hand-thrown earthenware. There were woven seats, solid, simply built oak tables, painted brick arches. Having been at Bedales, where crafts and craftsmanship were central to our education – we wove and made rugs, sculpted, made jewellery, studied bookbinding, made leather shoes, furniture – Cranks seemed like an extension of all the things I'd taken for granted were part of a civilised world and a civilised culture, though food, bizarrely, was never considered intrinsic to it. It always struck me as extraordinary that a school so concerned with educating the mind and the hands, the left – logos – and the right – intuitive – hemispheres of the brain, and where music and the arts were afforded their rightful place in the curriculum, should not consider the nurturing of mind and body with good food as essential to us, as human beings going out into the world, and a valid part of our cultural inheritance.

At Cranks, they preached on the plate, not a worthy, unimaginative religion of dull, bland, old-school food, but one that rebelled against the new industrialisation and the post-war move to processed and convenience foods. Cranks were rooted in the soil, the earth, proper agricultural principles but most importantly to taste, to simple food that was served as close as possible to how it was harvested. They believed in colour and texture to stimulate the senses and almost automatically guarantee a balanced diet.

This new 'hippy food' became the butt of much dismissive derision, the bran and the brown becoming synonymous with nut cutlets and lentil bakes and cardboard-thick wholewheat pastry. The simple philosophy of 'Nature knows best' that Cranks believed in, was somehow what my muddled, newly impassioned adolescent brain had alighted on and adhered to and no amount of parental or school influence could deflect it.

I had already begun to think through the connection between food and health, precipitated by my father becoming ill during my early teenage years and dying when I was 18. I had begun to think that I was responsible for my own health and that preventive medicine began with diet, with good food. Having the death of a parent to contend with, followed the next year by my mother's getting breast cancer, sent me searching for reasons, for knowledge, for information on the effects of drugs and drink and antibiotics and the possible effects of an unbalanced, over-processed and under-nutritious diet. My connection to nature and the principle of 'unus mundus' was budding, indeed, has never been shaken from the bough.

Cranks' two recipe books became as important to my simple philosophy of food as the other more exalted writers like Elizabeth David and Jane Grigson, and my children were brought up with their homity pies, banana yoghurt flan, many of their pulse-based main courses and wholewheat flour cakes, cookies and puddings. Yes, it resulted in the Mrs Organic label from all three children and their begging for something white from the chiller cabinet from time to time, but they have been brought up respecting the earth, good ingredients, farming principles, animal husbandry and good food in a far more educated way than when I was trying to work it all out for myself.

'Alternative' medicine was the next subject to creep into the collective consciousness, allied as it is, through herbs and a holistic approach, to the food we put into our mouths and how we look after our bodies. I made a series of documentaries for BBC2 on herbal medicine and homeopathy and became part of the new society that questioned the way medicine, healing and health were going. Again, these things that were so of their time, were linked in a way that we didn't discern at the time, but we now look on them as inter-connected, as mainstream and established, no longer outrageous, unscientific and 'out there'.

Another simple, unpretentious vegetarian restaurant opened in a dark, downstairs basement in the mid-'70s in Covent Garden, Food for Thought, using only ingredients of the best quality and piling up rainbow coloured foods with millet and wheat berries, barley and pasta, bakes and pies, wholewheat cheese baps spilling with cress, and vibrant vegetables. The cheapness and value for money had as much of an effect on me as a student as the nourishing soups and beany, tomatoey stews. Here were people who wanted to give value, thus meaning, to the food they cooked and to the people they were nourishing. Everything was unpretentious, an expression of exuberance and freedom on the plate and the use of fresh herbs and spices was a revelation.

A few months ago I was walking down Neal St and time came to as swift a halt as I did. There, through the door that opened onto a bustling kitchen staffed by people who looked more or less the same as 40 years ago, was the same staircase leading down to the same, simple wooden restaurant, serving food that looked somehow familiar though a little bit dissimilar.

Food for Thought has survived the food fashions and decades of change since its opening and is still going strong. I waited in line on the staircase and on arriving at the blackboard wanted everything on the menu from the roasted red pepper soup to the age-old wholewheat mushroom tart whose generous depth and heft clearly still adhered to past principles. The tart came with a lavish spoon of well-seasoned potato salad turned in good oil, lemon juice, herbs and spring onions, a butter bean salad, properly floury and leguminous and cut with fresh tomatoes and sprightly green herbs and a home-made raw slaw. The low tables were filled with people who were happily digging into deep plates and enjoying bounty, good value, freshness of flavour and preparation, and the love and care that go into that. My piled-high plate cost £8. It was better than many meals I have eaten costing eight times that.

I told Charissa about Food for Thought that evening, and the following day she went. She bought the book. She has started cooking their recipes. She can afford to go there, but goes there out of choice, not necessity. She has always been committed to their sort of food and philosophy and to its central place in her life.

Wholewheat pastry still makes me smile. I KNOW it isn't haute cuisine, I know it should be cut 50:50 with white flour for lightness and crispness, but re-living what first got me hooked on hippy food and adapting it with, perhaps, a degree more finesse, sophistication, technique than I first encountered, is still part of why and how I came to cook and eat good food made with good ingredients.

Nothing, yet everything has changed since these brave pioneers reinvented the wheel.

Since the daring days when so much of our freedom was spent experimenting with danger and not really understanding the consequences. But experimenting need not be harnessed to post-facto regret. Without daring to question and extend boundaries, pierce holes in received wisdom, without the subjectivity of our individual inherited personality traits, we would never, collectively, aspire or change or establish a new order.

We were oh, so lucky that we heeded not the strictures and structures that had begun to stagnate and ossify and fragment after post-war exhaustion and reconstruction, which didn't seem to have any contemporary relevance to our lives. Oh, so lucky, that we were there as witnesses, if not innovators to the sexes rediscovering each other in a newer and ultimately more powerfully connected way. And to rediscovering good food which is everyone's right.

. . . .

HOMITY PIES

The originals. And as good as ever they were in those heady Cranks days. My children may laugh, but I smile. Ritual has become tradition.

325g potatoes
30g butter
3–4 tbsp full cream milk
sea salt and pepper
450g onions, finely
    chopped
2 tbsp olive oil
2 cloves garlic, crushed
2 tbsp parsley, chopped,
    old-style, not flat-leaf
    if possible
120g very mature Cheddar
    like Montgomery, a
    good, unpasteurised
    cheese, not block
    Cheddar
2 large tomatoes, sliced

makes 20 cm/8 inch tart
    or 6 individual ones
serves 6

Preheat the oven to 180°C/Gas 4. Make the shortcrust pastry (see p.196) in the normal way, preferably with 50:50 wholewheat to plain flour, bake blind and dry out in the oven.

For the filling: boil the potatoes, drain them and mash them with the butter, milk and seasoning.

While they are cooking, sauté the onions over a medium heat in the olive oil until softened and translucent.

Stir into the mash with the crushed garlic, the parsley and ¾ of the cheese.

Fill the baked blind tart shells with the mixture, sprinkling on the rest of the cheese and adding a slice of tomato to each tart.

Bake in the oven for 20 minutes until gratineed, golden and bubbling.

Leave to cool on a rack and eat hot or warm.

Great wrapped in foil and eaten on a windy, west of Ireland beach.

WRAXALL TART, LEEK, BASIL, GRUYÈRE AND GOAT'S CHEESE

As one of the top-level pledgers to Smart Tart, Kay Ord *asked for her tart to reflect her kitchen garden. She also asked for Gruyère, which works particularly well with leeks, giving that yielding goo as you delve through the crust to the centre.*

I use some of the more tender green tops of the leeks which many waste; I think they add colour and flavour. I thought an ash log of Golden Cross unpasteurised goat's cheese which has always been a favourite of mine would work well here, and would hold its shape and form, which, as you can see from the picture, it did.

Here is a tart which a 50:50 wholewheat and plain flour crust works wonderfully well with, but the pastry is your choice.

30g butter
1 tbsp olive oil
5 medium leeks, cleaned, with the tender green tops kept, chopped
sea salt and white pepper
2 heaped tbsp basil
1 tbsp tarragon, optional
200 ml double cream
2 eggs + 2 yolks
90g Gruyère, Beaufort or Comté, grated
225g Golden Cross goat's cheese log or anything similar, as in a firm goat's cheese

makes 28 cm/11 inch tart
serves 8–10

Preheat the oven to 180°C/Gas 4. Make the shortcrust pastry in the normal way (see p.196), or with 50:50 wholewheat/plain flour. Bake blind and dry out in the oven.

For the middle: melt the butter with the olive oil in a large, heavy-bottomed frying pan, then throw in the leeks and leek tops, season and sauté gently until they begin to wilt and soften.

Remove from the heat and add the fresh herbs.

Whisk together the cream, eggs, seasoning and Gruyère.

Scrape the leeks into the cream.

Slice the goat's cheese and arrange around the edge of the tart, scrape in the leeky custard and bake for 35–40 minutes or until set and gloriously browned.

Cool on a rack for at least 15 minutes before turning out and eating.

TARTE A LA RIPPON

Adam Pepper is a super-pledger to Smart Tart, *who wanted a tarty present for Sam.*

Adam wanted his surname somewhere in the mix, so I suggested cracked peppercorns in the crust, which appealed. I favour white peppercorns, the best come from Sarawak, but please use black if you prefer.

Adam suggested some of Sam's favourite ingredients, Iberico ham – for which you may substitute Prosciutto if you prefer – Gruyère and tomatoes.

Here is the delectable result, I hope Sam and Adam have a feast.

1 dstsp white or black
    peppercorns
200 ml double cream
2 eggs + 2 yolks
sea salt
90g Gruyère
6 slices Iberico ham, or
    enough to lay on the
    pastry base
24 cherry or baby plum
    tomatoes, halved
2 tbsps chopped parsley

makes a 20 cm/8 inch tart,
    or 6 little individual
    ones like I did for the
    picture
serves 6

Preheat the oven to 180°C/Gas 4. Make the shortcrust pastry in the usual way (see p.196), with the following addition: 1 dstsp white or black peppercorns cracked in a mortar, the powder sieved out so that you just use the bits. Scatter them on your pastry when you roll it out.

For the filling: whisk the cream and eggs with a little sea salt and the Gruyère.

Lay the ham on the base of the pastry, straight out of the oven, then assemble the tomatoes all around and either scatter parsley all over, or keep it like a green crop circle in the middle of the tart or little tarts like I did.

Bake for 35–40 minutes if you have made a large tart, until golden brown, or check after 25 minutes with small tarts and remove when set and browned.

Cool on a rack for 15 minutes before turning out.

ROAST PUMPKIN, GOAT'S CROTTIN AND SAGE TART

This tart is an Irish tricolour of a tart, with the saffron pumpkin, green sage and white. You may make it with red onion squash or sweet potato if it suits, the roasting arrests any wateriness and strengthens the flavour, it also gives texture.

I added young sage leaves and their flowers, a vibrant purple, as it was that time of year and my sage bush was in flower.

Crottins are aged, so they crumble without disintegrating and have a characteristic fudgy saltiness, perfect for a tart.

about 225–250g pumpkin, red onion squash or sweet potato
a little olive oil
sea salt and pepper
a large handful/2 tbsps chopped sage
2 aged crottins
200 ml double cream
2 eggs + 2 yolks

makes a 20 cm/8 inch tart, or 6 individual ones
serves 6

Preheat the oven to 180°C/Gas 4. Make the shortcrust pastry in the usual way (see p.196), bake blind and dry out in the oven.

For the middle: peel and cube the pumpkin and toss in a small roasting tin with a little olive oil so they are coated. Season with sea salt and a little pepper.

Place in the oven to roast, they should take 15–20 minutes depending on the cube size, but remove when slightly al dente and browned.

Scatter the chopped sage over the pumpkin.

Break and crumble the crottins into small chunks.

Whisk the cream, eggs and seasoning.

Remove the tart from the oven and scrape the crottins and pumpkin mixture over the base then pour over the custard and return to the oven for 35–40 minutes for a large tart, check after 25 for individual tarts.

Remove when set, golden brown and puffed up and cool on a rack for at least 15 minutes.

Remember that it is as absurd to be surprised that the world brings forth the fruits with which it teems as that the fig-tree should bear figs.

Marcus Aurelius, *Meditations*

The fig. The beginning of civilisation as we know it. The world didn't commence with the fall of an apple, it began with the unfurling of a fig-leaf. Splayed like a hand, the lime-green fig-leaf became a symbol, the perfect protector of our modesty.

The fig is inextricably linked with The Fall, with sex, procreation and begetting; with innocence and experience, ripeness, spoiling and death. Quite a lot for this small, tender orb to take upon itself when you think about it.

Yet, the fig's real history begins well before Adam and Eve's fall from celestial grace left the Garden of Eden to its own devices and vices, choked with weeds, presumably, thorny, thicketed, brambly, boggy, and abundant in this soft-skinned fruit that over-ripens as fast as a purple-black bruise.

Its history dates back to at least 9440–9200 BC, from when we have nine sub-fossil figs, which were found in a Neolithic village in the Jordan valley. The find pre-dates the domestication of wheat, barley, legumes and may be the first known incidence of agriculture. That means the fig may just have been the first thing that man cultivated intentionally. Surely as extraordinary a human breakthrough as anything man has achieved scientifically or artistically.

Think about it. What kind of brain had developed in Man at this point? Man, who had thus far been unable to see, perhaps, the necessity, the benefit for us as a species. Of being able to survive better, longer, on food that cropped regularly, reliably and upon which we could gorge in abundance, fresh or dried, particularly when there were no other crops available?

It tells us of man's gene and genus for striving to put down roots and cultivate. Could it be that our early survival skills were also informed by an inherent sense of what our bodies needed? We must, at the point we began to cultivate, have observed the effects of different foods upon our growth, our health, our appetite. Even were it an unreasoned, inchoate craving, we must have intuited, connected, our survival, our strength, stamina, fitness with the various foods we ate that kept us alive.

Figs are amongst the richest food-source of calcium and fibre. If the herds providing milk and meat weren't obliging, figs would have provided these vital sources instead.

Dried figs are the richest source of fibre, high in copper, manganese, magnesium, potassium, vitamin K. Could the vagaries of available plant sources and animal protein have been supplemented with the fig, which, when dried, may have been crucial for a Nomadic people during the winter months. The laxative and anti-oxidant properties could also have contributed to the fig being an almost complete food. Added to this, its cropping twice a year, portability, yielding flesh easily eaten by the very young or those without teeth, its trees quick to grow and abundant in their fruiting.

Figs can grow in the heat of the desert and the severest chill of the mountains. The Persian wild fig, the 'Anjeer Kohi', needs no irrigation and survives a temperature of minus 40°C.

A fruit for all seasons, all ages, all places.

'Every fruit has its secret'

So D. H. Lawrence says in his poem 'Figs', it's just that figs are more secretive than most given the clandestine nature of their anatomy and the very femaleness they conceal beneath their curiously masculine exterior.

'It was always a secret.
That's how it should be, the female should always be secret.'

Lawrence describes, in extravagantly overt verse, the fruit in all her female intimacy, open to be eaten 'the proper way', split in four, or 'the vulgar way':

'Is just to put your mouth to the crack, and take out the flesh in one bite.'

Peeled, quartered, crushed, splayed, no-one would disagree, the fig is the most candid of fruits. Almost an embarrassment to eat in public as it reveals not just its own innermost nature, but so much about that of the person eating it. T. S. Eliot's 'The Love of J. Alfred Prufrock' captured this private/public moment in his 'Do I dare to eat a peach?'

Green, purple or black-skinned, all figs have a similar plush-lined crimson interior with a characteristic tobacco-ey, grainy crunch. The milky-white sap that exudes when you cut or bite reminds me of the sap of a dandelion leaf that bleeds white when you tear it, though the fig hasn't the dandelion's bitter heart.

However sweet and mild the fig is eaten warm from the tree, I think figs are best served with lactic ricotta and Prosciutto or a sharp, lemon and mint cream dressing; turned into pretty pink ice cream, baked briefly in a hot oven with a squirl of Prosciutto fat melting into them and a sprinkle of thyme; roasted en papillote with a black pudding stuffed fillet of pork and Marsala.

Figs have a broad canvas on which to paint your brushstrokes. Simply baked with rich, raw chestnut honey, crushed walnuts and Marsala or with raspberries pushed into their opened petals or dribbled with raspberry puree – a brilliant way with a fig tart – the pastry brushed with melted white chocolate to keep it crisp, the fig lends complex texture and subtle flavour to sweet, salt, sharp, smoky and creamy and brings a tender, sensuality to everything it touches.

One is never enough.

Two rarely is.

Three, and you're at risk of their laxative effect unless they're accompanied by pork.

Burrata sits happily next to a plate of figs, the two salted and sprinkled with mellow, aged, velvety balsamic.

What versatility.

In the winter, the sticky, seeded richness of the dried fig comes into its own. A dried fruit compote studded with Hunza or unsulphured apricots, prunes, figs and lemon peel with a warming spice or two makes a perfect breakfast. You can add almonds, hazelnuts, walnuts, toasted or untoasted, yoghurt and runny honey.

A figgy pudding dense with nuts and dried fruit and raisins is less rich at Christmas.

A dried fig ice cream with nuggets of the fruit and pralineed bashed up almonds, a little orange zest and Oloroso sherry is dreamy.

Or just stick with a fig leaf and a whiter than white, innocent little fresh goat's cheese plonked on top of it for earthy elegance and simplicity.

O, the felicitous fig.

.......................:...................

ANTIPASTI TARTS

I am not giving you a serves 8, 10, 30 here as it is entirely up to you how many individual tarts you make and whether you decide to serve them with drinks, as a starter, a lunch or a supper dish. And you must combine as you see fit, you don't have to make the complete range that you can see in the picture.

All I can say is that these mouthfuls of buttery-crisp puff pastry decked with the best fresh ricotta, Prosciutto-wrapped asparagus, olives, herbs, tomatoes, are breathtakingly easy and quick to assemble and as hot tarts go, they went. One sheet of puff pastry (see p.198) makes 15 tarts if you cut them out with a tumbler-sized glass.

So, for 15:

1 sheet all butter puff pastry

Any or all of the following:

3 cloves garlic

250g fresh ricotta

sea salt and pepper

6 slices Prosciutto

a small bunch of basil, chopped

a small bunch of mint, chopped fine

4 spears cooked, cooled asparagus, the tips only

½ crottin

2 tbsps black olives, chopped

1 doz cherry or small tomatoes, halved

2 figs, sliced

olive oil, a good fruity one

Preheat the oven to 200°C/Gas 6. Place the discs of puff pastry on a greased baking sheet and prick with a fork.

Crush the garlic into the fresh ricotta, season, then divide the ricotta into two.

Tear up a couple of slices of Prosciutto small and turn them into one of the blobs of ricotta.

Add half of the chopped basil to the ricotta and Prosciutto mixture, half the mint to the garlicky ricotta.

Roll a small piece of Prosciutto around the asparagus spears.

Place a good dessertspoon of the two ricotta mixtures on each disc of pastry leaving a little edge free.

Add a few tiny bits of crottin, olives and tomatoes to some of the basil blobs, a sliced fig to some of the minted ones, the wrapped asparagus to some of the basil blobs.

Dribble over a little of the olive oil and bake for 15 minutes. Check their progress after 12 minutes.

When crisped and brown and well puffed up around the edges, remove from the oven and place on a rack.

After a couple of minutes, slip the tarts onto the rack to cool for 5 minutes. Before serving warm, dribble on a little more oil and the rest of the herbs.

FIG, RASPBERRY AND WHITE CHOCOLATE TART

This summer dream of a tart is made entirely with raw fruit. The raw raspberry puree hidden beneath the figs is sharp, bright, and a total complement to the seedy, sweet figs. The white chocolate is a perfect barrier that comes between the pastry and the raspberry to stop the pastry sogging and to add a final hidden, unexpected sweetness.

A showstopper of a tart.

400g raspberries – keep a few back to decorate the top of the tart with

2 tbsp unrefined icing sugar

a spritz of lemon

70g white chocolate very gently melted

10–12 figs

2 heaped tbsp redcurrant jelly and a tsp water to glaze

makes 26 cm/10 inch tart serves 8–10

Preheat the oven to 180°C/Gas 4. Make the sweet crust or sablée pastry in the usual way (see p.198), bake blind then continue to cook until baked through, for another 15 minutes. Test by touch. Cool on a rack.

Meanwhile, make the middle: blitz 350g or so of the raspberries in the Magimix with the icing sugar, then sieve them into a bowl and taste. Spritz with a little lemon juice to bring out the flavour. The puree should be sharp.

Melt the white chocolate by heating a small pan until the base is hot, removing from the heat and throwing in the chocolate off the heat.

When it is still warm and before it hardens, brush a good layer of white chocolate over the cooled pastry and allow it to set.

Scrape the raspberry puree over the chocolate.

Arrange the figs in whatever way suits your artistic nature. Likewise the remaining raspberries.

Melt the redcurrant jelly and when liquid, brush it over the fruit to glaze. Best served chilled, as in after an hour or so in the fridge.

Note: If you can't find figs or prefer apricots, poach 20–24 of them in a couple of glasses of white or rosé wine with 2 strips lemon peel, 1 tbsp light muscovado sugar and the scraped out seeds and pod of a vanilla pod. When al dente remove with a slotted spoon and decorate the tart with apricots and raspberries, serving the jug of poaching liquor alongside. I made this in France recently where I couldn't find redcurrant jelly, but substituted it with delicate rose petal jelly for the glaze.

FAMINE

12 FAMINE

When I was a child, there was still a burial mound – a famine grave – on Thallabawn. Set way back on the right of the deserted strand, towards the unevenly stitched patchwork of small fields and tumbly stone walls that abut it on all sides, it rose like a lightless beacon over the landscape reminding the local community of things they would probably rather not be reminded of. This tower of sand, held tightly together by the sharp, dune grasses and the rocks and sand from which it was formed, like a naked, exposed sculpture, never diminished in size despite the sand and wind ripping with the tides across the empty strand like an impassive, destructive force.

Nature bears witness impassively, even to unimaginable human disaster enacted at its midst.

In the years between 1845–1849 when the potato famine decimated the Irish people, and more than a million died of starvation, the north-west and Co. Mayo in the west of Ireland were the worst affected areas. Remote, wild, and where, despite official census figures, many more than those recorded lived in cabins in the boggy hills, backs of mountains and silent, isolated valleys, a peasantry already more destitute than any other in Europe, their women and children scattered, as Cecil Woodham-Smith writes in *The Great Hunger*, 'like a flock of famished crows over the fields devouring raw turnips'.

The combination of death and emigration meant that the population of Ireland was reduced from eight to four million, with Mayo losing over a quarter of its people. I cannot write this without feeling the horror of it: that these statistics occurred on our doorstep, in a land and sea of plenty, but that that plenty was beyond the reach of the 130,000 paupers who were tenant farmers on less than an acre and the grain they grew had to pay the rent to their Irish or British landlords to avoid their being evicted. When the potatoes failed, they had nothing.

Travelling up the north side of Killary, Ireland's only fjord, by boat from Bundorragha, with my old friend John Kilcoyne who keeps mussel rafts on the south side, we have moored and climbed the un-peopled hillside on the south face of Mweelrea, Connacht's highest mountain, with his wife Merci and my three children. Here the echoes of the famine resound most deeply, most silently in the deserted Derry village, abandoned during 'An Gorla Mor' – the great hunger – and now no more than a grid of stones and grey fallen walls, green, lichened and mossy chimney breasts imploded back into the land, surrounded by the corrugated ridges, all grassed over but still visible, where the potatoes grew until the blight turned them black, pulpy, rotten and inedible.

Looking out across Killary to its southern shore from here, you can see the Green Road with its meandering stone wall built on the sheer hillside as part of the famine relief project to reward labour with food. Since so many people were too ill or starving to work, the women were sent out rock-breaking and the children stone clearing. All these schemes were unproductive as the government didn't want to upset the chances of profit from private developers. The road, the wall, were built going nowhere.

We walk this southern side of Killary too, in the summer, to the far end of the wall, over the hill and down to the small village of Rosroe where the Viennese philosopher Wittgenstein stayed after World War II and completed his second major work, Philosophical Investigations. Wittgenstein must have walked this same walk many times, passing the long-deserted settlement of Foher and its sad secrets to the open mouth of Killary Harbour which yawns wide into the open sea with the island of Inis Bofin directly ahead.

All around my Mayo house, high into the Six Noggins – the hills on the bog side to the north – and as far as swallow-fly to the sea, across commonage, fields, headland, these now grassed, defunct potato ridges cover every inch of ground, etched like a woodcut across each fold and hillock, a living memory of the land's past, its cultivation returned to wildness.

Wherever you walk you are walking over the bones of the dead. In the worst affected areas, where no-one was strong enough to dig a shallow grave, bodies were simply stacked, bone on stone, sand on bone; where interment could take place the dead were buried in mass pits and where the soil was loosest on the sea borders like Thallabawn, the dogs would have feasted first before the bones lay exposed to sun, sea, sand, rain, ruin.

Thinking about it now, I am troubled by the fact that we sheltered against the burial mound as children, with our parents, spreading our picnics out on the sand, tins filled with sandwiches – meat, cheese, jam – slabs of sticky black fruit cake, oranges, apples, bananas and bars of Cadbury's Golden Crisp and ate with our own great hunger, that of children in the salt sea air, in the shadow of so much death. We climbed the mound as though it were a sandy turret. As though it were there for our amusement.

Returning a little over a decade later with my three young children, the mound had been swept away. That it should have remained intact for over 140 years may have suggested a permanence that anything written in sand would disavow. It was as though the collective will of the bones of the dead had kept tenure so that future generations would remember and learn from the past, until the winds had simply blown it from the memory of the land.

Stooping down, I found a bog-black skull part-buried in the sand. Dislodged, displaced, in life, in death, I couldn't leave it for further sands and gales to blow through its empty sockets, for above ground is for the living, or so we are taught.

I took it back to my land above, almost fearing the consequences.

Would the soul of this poor skull cast a spell over us?

Is there such a thing as residual sorrow?

You would believe there was if you walked or drove the Doo Lough Pass between Louisburgh and Delphi Lodge at the southern tip of Doo Lough (the black lake) the other side of Mweelrea from me.

Enclosed by mountains rising skywards from the edges of the lough on all sides, the Doolough Pass is a solitary, hemmed-in wilderness with no houses for several miles. Cloud descends into the eerie, dark basin of mountain on one side of the lake and sits like steam in a dark cauldron; streams are precipitated by the sudden rainstorms that make this one of the wettest places in Ireland and then the slate and granite glistens wet and shiny, black and silver and new waterfalls gush from jagged rocks right down to the godforsaken road in its hewed-out loneliness.

William Carleton in *The Black Prophet*, his famine novel of 1847, described the 'fearful desolation' he had encountered in the western parishes, and in this particular one, what happened on this road made it the road to hell.

On the night of Friday 30th March, 1849, two officials, Col. Holgrove and Capt. Primrose were due to arrive in Louisburgh to inspect those in receipt of outdoor relief, which meant they could claim their small ration of meal. The two men didn't stop, they went on to Delphi 12 miles south, where they instructed the crowds to appear at 7 a.m. on the 31st if they wanted to continue receiving relief.

Hundreds of skeletal, destitute, starving people walked in vengeful weather, 'famished with the cold', as they say in Mayo, and waited outside the Delphi gates. There was driving rain, bitter wind, sleet and snow freezing and drenching those who walked what has come to be known as 'the death march' in their rags, sunken eyed, hollow cheeked, desperate. They were turned away and began the walk back to Louisburgh along the side of Doo Lough, the sickest falling over, some buried where they fell if there was enough soil to cover them, others swept into the lough by heavy squalls. Some say that almost 400 people, starving adults and children, never reached home, that many were found lying with grass in their mouths they were so hungry, dying where they dropped.

I have climbed all these mountains since my childhood, and continue to do so, and swum in the icy black depths of Doo Lough with my father, my brother, my children. We have climbed up the waterfall on the northern end of Doo Lough towards the sea, setting off from a track that led to a tiny farm where the Gavins lived until relatively recently, two old brothers and a sister, out on a limb of hillside invisible from the road, buried behind the mouth of the lough. They would run from the sheep pens, from dipping or shearing and cross the little bridge to greet us when we walked up their path, as though any sign of life other than sheep demanded celebration.

Driving the road from Leenane through Delphi towards the small scattering of houses and derelict school at Cregganbaum on the Louisburgh road at night is an unsettling experience. With the tar-black lough on your left, moonlight does nothing to still the fear, the ripples on the lake-face glitter with Gothic menace, and if there is no moon, you are alone in a landscape that bears down on you and crowds you in the way that enclosed valleys do, making you want to scream and get out into open space.

Charissa and I say the same thing each time: suppose we were to breakdown here at the lough edge, would we walk, or would we stay in the car until the grey dawn chased the night terror away, leaving us feeling stupid and irrational 'the soul becomes dyed with the colour of its thoughts' Marcus Aurelius said, and fear stains deep.

The Irish have no word for being alone; in Gaelic they say 'liom fein' – I am with myself – nowhere more so than in this still desolate part of Mayo, where we are not alone, we are alone with nature, at one with nature. We can admit to feeling physically how the landscape has been penetrated with sadness because the world is not divisible like we once believed it to be, 21st-century science has finally acknowledged the limitations of the mechanistic view of the world it held since the 17th century.

As we penetrate into matter, nature appears as a complicated web of relations between the various parts of a unified whole. This cosmic web of relations includes the human observer and his consciousness in an essential way. We can never speak about nature without, at the same time, speaking about ourselves.

What a brave and brilliant revelation from the mind of the 20th-century genius Fritjof Capra, who wrote *The Tao of Physics*, in his Schumacher lecture 'Buddhist Physics'. The idea that modern physics, 'once the manifestation of an extreme specialisation of the rational mind, is now making contact with mysticism – the essence of religion – and the manifestation of the extreme specialization of the intuitive mind, shows beautifully the unity and complementary nature of the rational and intuitive modes of consciousness.'

Exactly what you feel intuitively in this place, for what is written into the DNA of the landscape makes it feel like it contains past energy, the people who came before; the place has stored and now reflects the things that happened to those people if you are only open to thinking and feeling and absorbing these truths.

The famine had, I believe, another legacy. The generosity of the families on the stretch of Mayo coast where I have my house is about giving and sharing food, be it the day's catch of mackerel and coal fish from one of their currachs, or freshly dug sweet carrots, onions, lettuces, squeaky green cabbages and potatoes. Eggs from the hens, ducks or turkeys, tea and cake, pots of home-made blackcurrant jam, you cannot enter a house without being offered something to eat and drink, and no-one comes visiting without bringing something from the sea or the land or freshly baked.

Perhaps the gift of food has become the unspoken reminder of the famine in these times where Ireland is seeing history repeat itself with a new wave of emigration of the young since the recession.

I have noticed several neighbours going back to planting vegetables, even though the house pig and cow, making black pudding, churning the butter, the daily baking of a cake of soda bread, all of which were common ten years ago, have still to be revitalised. I have no doubt they will be, time has not been so long passing that these traditional skills have been lost by a generation devoted to packets and processed, particularly in a rural economy so deeply affected by the small-scale economies of the land.

However cruelly the current recession digs into the heart of this place, and however many leave its shores, the quality of life has changed spectacularly since famine times. Compare this sweep of emigrants to those poor, half-starved souls who left in the mid-19th century, many dying of cholera and typhoid on the way to America, and look at the land now: flocks of sheep and cattle everywhere, vegetables flourishing in the sandy, seaweedy soil, cheese makers in Westport, currant bushes, apple and rowan trees surviving the Atlantic gales, oysters in Clew Bay, mussel rafts the length of Killary, herring, lobsters, crabs.

Those who return to their family farms will have toughed it out in Australia, New Zealand, America like generations before them; they will return to a place that remains forever undefeated by tragedy or disaster and whose people will roll with the cycle of reinvention once more, just with better ideas, better tools and the indomitable Mayo spirit that is a match for both the land and the landscape.

..................:..................

TORTA DELLA NONNA

It seems fitting that a tart that any self-respecting Italian household – and, I am sure, ALL Italian 'nonnas', grandmothers, would make with ingredients always to hand, of the most basic, yet delicious kind – should fall at the end of this chapter, Famine. Curious how well chocolate, a tiny scattering of grated, traditionally, but in my case I have melted it for a twist, should pair so well with lemon zest.

You may decide to do what I did, make extra crème patisserie and a glazed strawberry tart at the same time. It is not traditional to make a crème patisserie with lemon peel, so make yours without if you feel like it.

500 ml whole milk, preferably Jersey or Channel Islands

finely pared zest of 1 lemon in 4–5 strips, peeled with a potato peeler

1 split vanilla pod, the seeds scraped out

90g unrefined granulated sugar

4 large egg yolks

2 tbsp cornflour

small knob of butter, walnut sized

60–90g pine nuts

30–45g dark chocolate

makes 20 cm/8 inch tart, or 8 individual ones.

serves 8

Preheat the oven to 180°C/Gas 4. Make the sweet crust or sablée pastry in the normal way (see p.198), bake blind, then dry out in the oven.

Meanwhile, make the filling: warm the milk in a heavy-bottomed pan with the lemon peel and vanilla pod and seeds and half the sugar.

Whisk the egg yolks in a large bowl with the remaining sugar, then whisk in the cornflour.

Pour in a little of the hot milk, whisking as you go to keep the mixture smooth, then whisk in the remaining milk and pour the whole lot back into the pan and place it over the heat.

Whisk until thickened, then remove the peel and pod.

Pour the custard back into the bowl and add the butter in small pieces.

Cool until just warm.

Spoon the custard into the cooked pastry case then chill in the fridge for a couple of hours.

When ready to serve, toast the pine nuts in a small, dry frying pan until oily and biscuit coloured and scatter them on top of the tart.

Melt the chocolate and spatter the top with it, or grate chocolate on top.

STRAWBERRY TART

It is impossible to resist the window of a proper French village patisserie with its array of fruit tarts redly glazed and gleaming and the custard peeking through. Use any fruit you wish, but don't cook it, the whole point is 'au naturel' with whatever is in season, raspberries, blackberries, apricots or redcurrants, but most of all strawberries.

....

500 ml whole milk, preferably Jersey or Channel Islands

finely pared zest of 1 lemon in 4–5 strips, peeled with a potato peeler

1 split vanilla pod, the seeds scraped out

90g unrefined granulated sugar

4 large egg yolks

2 tbsp cornflour

small knob of butter, walnut sized

....

makes 20 cm/8 inch tart, or 8 individual ones.

serves 8

Preheat the oven to 180°C/Gas 4. Make a sweet crust or pâté sablée pastry (see p.198) and bake blind then cook until baked through for a further 15 minutes. Touch test. Place on a rack to cool.

Meanwhile, make the filling: warm the milk in a heavy-bottomed pan, with or without the lemon peel, and vanilla pod and seeds and half the sugar.

Whisk the egg yolks in a large bowl with the remaining sugar, then whisk in the cornflour.

Pour in a little of the hot milk, whisking as you go to keep the mixture smooth, then whisk in the remaining milk and pour the whole lot back into the pan and place it over the heat.

Whisk until thickened, then remove the peel and pod.

Pour the custard back into the bowl and add the butter in small pieces.

Cool until just warm.

When the tart case has cooled and the crème patisserie is warm, scrape it into the tart shell and chill.

Before serving decorate with roughly 1 kg strawberries and then glaze with 2 tbsps redcurrant melted with a tsp of water.

13 MATTERS OF THE HEART

The best diet is to fall in love. Have you ever been thinner, happier, more anxious, more stricken with fear, more alive, less hungry? You can't look at food. You can't eat in front of the *innamorato*, you can just try and look beautiful.

No, that is not quite true.

The really best diet is having your heart broken. You never notice not eating, you feel sick, nauseous, empty – with grief, not hunger – your heart crushed and racing in your chest, palpitating, out of control, its beat louder than a clock (it skips beats but doesn't strike the hour).

It is wonderful and terrible, like being off-piste map-less in an avalanche; consumed, every waking hour – and the few you manage to sleep – in fear of not hearing from the object of your affection, in a fug of unknowing, in fear for your future, your sanity, your life.

You dream, you see the future together and as quickly tell yourself that's crazy love talking and it'll never happen.

You don't know where your uncontrolled thoughts come from, you can't press the STOP button, you are temporarily held hostage, though not against your will, begging for it all to stop, begging for it never to stop.

You know that when you land on calmer shores, the early stages of bliss and oblivion cannot be recaptured, can only be remembered, after you have begun to make history together: so you have to live in the moment, because all of the above was the irrational self-seeing and believing only the beautiful thoughts, the good and beautiful person.

It is the irrational that governs that strange, pumping embodiment of love, the heart.

If the pharmaceutical companies invented a drug that mimicked the extreme states of the love spectrum, the obesity crisis would vanish overnight.

In America that would lead to $150 billion slashed from wasted health care. I'm sure we are the per capita equivalent, as America, Australia and England are up at the top of the greasy obesity pole.

There really isn't, to my mind, any difference between these two extreme states of falling in love and loss of love in terms of their psychological and physiological effects on us and our bodies, it's just that we have conveniently separated off and discarded their connection to each other and to our health in this age of pure reason.

Well, we'd better get the connection back, and begin to understand what we need to know to keep the heart happy and healthy, after all, we have a finite amount of heartbeats and we don't know when our heart is going to stop.

And we're making a pretty poor job of enhancing life expectancy given how much we now know, scientifically, evidentially, but choose to ignore or allow the food industry to lie to us about.

As we begin to understand neuroscience and the physiology of the brain better, I believe we are bound to become more enlightened on how inextricably linked brain chemistry and the emotions of the heart are, and what part food plays in the patterns, the harmonies and dissonances of both.

This isn't as crazy as you may think. There have been studies on what a brain in love looks like as seen through an fMRI machine which maps neural activity by measuring changes in blood flow. Individuals who were deeply in love viewed images of their beloved and simultaneously had their brains scanned, and literal fireworks of colour across the grey-matter showed that love activates in the caudate nucleus via a flood of dopamine.

Romance isn't the only thing that stimulates increases in dopamine, nicotine and cocaine follow the same pattern. Dopamine is released, we feel good, we want more. Like dopamine; like chocolate. As far as the brain is concerned, you are an addict. If you don't get the reward you want, i.e. you are lovelorn, stricken, and look at a picture of the object of your affections, the brain's neurons don't just shut down because the reward isn't coming, they keep going and waiting for a fix. If you give up chocolate you obsess about it, you can't stop thinking about it, you are far more likely to give in and pig out on it than if you allowed yourself a little. You need a little fix!

Our bodies still react to physical and emotional threats like they did in cavemen times. Adrenalin surges through the body. Blood pressure rises. Breathing speeds up. Muscles contract. The digestion slows down, causing cramp, diarrhoea, constipation, nausea, vomiting. Making us vulnerable to physical illness.

Falling in love and broken-heart syndrome are characterised by these extreme changes in our bodies as well as our brains, and science, specifically images of our brains, reveal that these metaphors aren't just poetic flights of fancy. The neural circuitries of physical and emotional pain have evolved to alert us to danger. Love is dangerous. Loss is dangerous. Do we know how to listen to our bodies and our hearts? Do we know how to nurture and heal them?

Everyone knows that they actually feel the pain of heartbreak in their chest, their stomach, a dull ache, a piercing pain, a crushing sensation. When we say 'love hurts', it really does. Scientists believe that it's because the heart's accelerators and brakes are pushed simultaneously and the conflicting actions create the sensation of heartbreak. The hurt, as far as your brain is concerned, is no different from a stab wound.

Falling in love alters the brain too. We feel a sense of thrilling dependency, we look at the world differently through our own eyes and we glimpse the world through the eyes of another. We change our habits. We develop new rituals, eat new and different foods, are exposed to new ideas, landscapes, people. We reconstruct the brain, our emotions, and we remap our small world to include the other person. We intuit from first memory, our connection in the womb with our mother and the oneness we once felt and we try to reinvent it. Our bodies and our brains remember, our hearts feel.

Food and love improve our health if they are good and healthy foods and good love. It shows in our brain, the scanned brains of long, happily married couples actually evidence calm in the sites equated with fear and anxiety, just holding hands eases our response to stress and improves our health, we alter one another's physiology and neural functions.

I think this is a revelation. It is the strongest clue as to how we should live our lives; how we should love, eat to live and cook and eat with love. It grounds what could be seen to be a whimsical and slightly airy-fairy notion in fact and substance and sense. And in the senses. It is a holistic blueprint of both the microcosmic and macrocosmic picture of our lives, refers us back to my chapter Famine and all the thinking that was going on with Fritjof Capra and Schumacher.

Let's take it a little further towards a logical, but also an intuitive conclusion.

The stage I have got to in my life and my cooking life, the philosophical point where I stand now, has come from much experience and experiment, both rational and technical and enquiry-based: historical, anthropological, ethnic, indigenous, through familial observation on the one hand and through gut feeling, as in the Revolution chapter, on the other. The side my logical brain dismissed for decades and which I am now repairing, or trying to rewire, so that the two operate in tandem.

As I learned to cook, and thought and read more and more on the subject of food, as I have watched and reflected on others' poor and good, refined and unrefined eating habits and their awareness or lack of it of their health, their brain, their bodies, I have connected up many small yet significant conclusions that have led me to larger ones and to beliefs. They are personal, but more than personal, they have a universal element.

You can only listen to your body and know what it needs, rather than craves, if you have a finely tuned understanding and knowledge of the possible importance of the *terroir* you live in and why those foods that grow in it are probably the ones your body needs: the seasons; the lack of, or effect of food substances on you at varying times of the year; your shifts in weight, mood, spirits, health, well-being.

You have to watch yourself over repeated years and also refer back to an innate wisdom and knowledge I believe is stored in your own DNA and probably has been since cavemen times. We are all in danger of not listening to it, of falling under the spells of the food giants, industrialisation, the city – which doesn't function in the same way as the country and which disconnects us from the land that feeds us. Of not listening to our bodies and our souls, instead we press override with our intellects which we see as superior.

I have pared down my cooking and made it entirely based on the purest ingredients I can find, as few of them as marry harmoniously, with as little done to them as possible. To as few processed foods as possible. Opting for simplicity has been a complex process in itself, as the nature of youth is to experiment and try everything and to add rather than subtract.

But simplicity in all things is something we return to, is a key to an inner door through which we left but must also return; is a metaphor for how to conduct a successful relationship.

Our relationship with food is a part of this process. Sharing food is, and always has been, a ritual act; it is sacred in all cultures. It seems sacrilegious to me that while we worry about huge sections of the world being underfed, starving, the truth is, more of the world is overfed. There are 30% more obese people than malnourished people worldwide. What resources we have to feed this uncontrollably growing planet are often wasted, spoiled, thrown back in the sea, don't reach their destination, are chucked away, don't maximise land usage but maximise profit.

We rear too many cattle who consume too much water, on too much grazing land, so that our emergent middle-class societies can buy more meat.

People eat quantities of carbohydrates laced with fructose and corn syrup, becoming obese while malnourished, saying they can't afford the right food, vegetables, fruit, protein. In fact they could afford them if they ate less and ate better and would consequently be healthier.

How could we lose all sense and knowledge of food and cooking in a generation?

It doesn't make sense to me. I cannot begin to understand it. But the chill words 'natural selection' spring to mind if we really make fools of ourselves in this way and are immune to the consequences.

A generation ago it was 'eat less fat'. We ate less fat. We ate stupid lean meats laced with sugar and salt to make them taste, skinless chicken breasts, and not enough unpasteurised cheese and dairy which we were told were bad for us. Erroneous. The food industry had played another trick on us. Instead, we multiplied our sugar consumption so dramatically that we didn't lose weight with less fat, we didn't get healthier, we got sicker and fatter and spawned a generation of diabetics.

No government wants to make sensible laws about what can and can't be done *vis-à-vis* food processing as the farming industry and the food conglomerates are too powerful and it doesn't win elections. Corn syrup, sugar, fizzy drinks, fructose sugar separated from the fruit itself and its good fibre, the hidden sugars that lurk in almost everything. If you look at Dr Lustig from the University of California's films about this scourge on our health, you will see where the land lies.

You will also see where we need to return to.

If we go back to fundamentals, to the principles of love and good food, simplicity, goodness, the symbolic act of breaking bread and sharing wine together and sitting round a table with a simple supper and those we love around it, we won't go wrong. The problem is, how far we have travelled from what makes us unique and human whilst believing it an advance for civilisation.

It is, for once, a pretty simple problem to solve for most of us and one that isn't beyond us on a global scale if the right energy, heart and brainpower are used to address it and the will is there.

..................:..................

BAKED RICOTTA, LEMON AND VANILLA TART

The rewards of trial and error, and more error, were finally won with this silken, ivory, custardy-set tart of infinite beauty and taste. I overcooked the first few attempts, which is all too easy to do, as I didn't trust the wobble and just carried on cooking. I now know better so will be firm with you, firm equals trembling. Also, I hadn't used fresh ricotta or got the right proportion of sharpness, which meant adding some lemon juice not just zest. This is a truly splendid summer tart best served cooled to a breath of warmth, just the memory of it really. Chilling alters the texture and flavour and it is not quite so good.

650g just under 3 x 250g fresh ricotta

200g mascarpone

2 heaped tbsp soured cream

150 ml Jersey or good double cream

90g vanilla caster sugar

1 egg + 1 yolk

zest of 2 lemons and juice of ½–1, to taste

1–2 tsp vanilla extract, more than you would expect

makes 24 cm/9½ inch tart
serves 8–10

Preheat the oven to 180°C/Gas 4. Make a sweet crust or pâte sablée pastry in the normal way (see p.198), bake blind and dry out in the oven.

Meanwhile, make the filling: remove the fresh ricotta from its muslin or packaging, making sure that as much of the whey has drained away as possible.

Place the ricotta in the Kitchen Aid or food processor with the mascarpone, soured cream, Jersey cream, sugar, eggs, zest and vanilla extract and process until smooth.

Remove the bowl, add the juice of half a lemon, fold in, taste, add more if you need to, likewise with the vanilla.

Scrape the mixture into the baked blind tart case and bake in the oven for 35 minutes before checking. It should be very shuddery in the middle. Give it another 5 minutes, then hold your nerve and remove and allow to cool completely to room temperature on a rack before turning out.

It really doesn't matter if it has a 'sad' centre; overcooked ricotta gets a claggy, over-baked texture and the silken smooth is what you are striving for.

WALNUT TART

No book of mine is complete without a recipe from my cousin Deborah, with whom I have enjoyed many a table from our childhood days at our mutual grandparents', through the raising of our children and to the far-flung places we have travelled to together over the years. Mostly on culinary missions.

Here is my version of the walnut tart recipe that she gave me which is very, very good and as rich as the rich-list.

Deborah serves it with home-made coffee ice cream, as did I. But crème fraîche is another way to go.

I made a 23 cm/9 inch square tart as you can see from the picture, but a circle of the same is just as good.

100 ml single cream
200g unsalted butter
a good pinch of sea salt
140g liquid glucose (good supermarkets sell it by the tube)
300g vanilla caste sugar
75 ml water
300g walnuts

makes 23 cm/9 inch tart
serves 10 (as it is
    jaw-droppingly rich)

Preheat the oven to 180°C/Gas 4. Make the sweet crust or pâté sablée pastry in the usual way but don't cook it (see p.198), the beauty of this tart is that it doesn't need baking blind.

Then make the middle: bring the cream and butter to scald-point, just below boiling point, in a pan over a medium heat. Add the salt.

Put the glucose, sugar and water into a heavy-bottomed frying pan and bring to a bubble, then carry on cooking without stirring until the bubbling mass seethes and browns to mahogany.

Remove from the heat and pour in the cream and butter mixture, watch out, it will splutter, and then immediately add the walnuts and stir.

Pour the mixture directly into the tart shell and bake until browned and set, 30–40 minutes. If you have any pastry left over, lattice strips placed quickly over the mixture with an egg-wash painted on before the tart goes into the oven works a treat.

Cool on a rack, turn out and chill. Serve straight from the fridge, the tart will have set more solidly.

the best restaurant

14 THE BEST RESTAURANT

The word 'restaurant' used to mean a place where you did, literally, go to restore yourself (*The Oxford Dictionary of Etymology* definition includes 'establishment for the provision of refreshments or meals. 1765; earlier in the sense "restorative"'), and I don't think that element should escape the proprietor if he or she takes his or her business seriously.

A restaurant is never only about the food, it is, at best, a place that makes you feel at home; the question is, what makes you feel at home? And the answer is, it's different for all of us.

The best watering holes make you feel like a valued and important guest, not overwhelmed, but in a low-key, personal way. Your coat is taken, you are shown directly to a table that is well spaced from the next so that you don't spend your whole lunch falling into next door's more gripping conversation; the linen is crisp, the table is clean and precisely laid, you are offered a drink, good bread – a fundamental – and the smiles of the staff are genuine, the staff are people, not ciphers, happy and proud to be doing their job, and don't mind if you order tap water, one course and look like you've just come in off the street. You have. They want you to be happy, relaxed, at ease and leave saying you can't wait to come back.

So. They don't say 'everything is good' when you ask for advice on what to order, or try to make you drink more than you wish to, and they don't interrupt. You are there to have a conversation and eat, not to constantly have your temperature checked and to be asked whether you are happy with the food.

If they're doing their job right, you won't feel intimidated about saying if you are not happy with something and not fearful that if you do, the kitchen will wreak a painful and hazardous revenge.

The staff should know never to say that 'the chef was happy with your dish' or that 'no-one else has complained and we have served 300 crème brûlées this week'. Both of which I've experienced in places that should know better. Which means everywhere. The former was a dish of 'rose rose veal' which I assumed was rose veal cooked in rosé wine. It was rose veal bathed in rose scented bubble bath. I offered a forkful to my daughter Miranda, I was so shocked by the taste, and she gagged. The latter was in Aix-en-Provence where I was treated like an ignorant British tourist who clearly didn't know what a crème brûlée should look or taste like. Mine had a gritty layer of completely unbrûléed white sugar as thick as the head on a pint of Guinness that meant it was like crunching neat granulated sugar and cream.

Charm school and the *Corps Diplomatique* come to mind with the best staff and maître d's, and certainly with sommeliers who have to deal with many more ignoramuses than they do Masters-of-wine. Looking down your reddled, Margaux-swollen nose at the would-be wine buff is not on, particularly in a three-star Michelin establishment where the sommeliers have much more to prove, in terms of not being intimidating.

I can forgive almost anything if the smiling, willing service makes me feel welcome. Forgetting, spilling, tardiness are all assuaged by grace under pressure and a 100-watt smile.

Lunch out, dinner out, is a treat for most people, even if they do it regularly. You want to feel the author's touch, the chef's mark in the dining room, after all, it is he whom you can't see in the engine room driving the ship and setting its course. If he doesn't attend to his staff up on deck it reflects upon the customer, how could it not? Simple: yes. Difficult: extremely, to pull off professionally, personally.

If the chef doesn't understand that the guest often comes back for the comfort of sameness, for a favourite dish, a friendly waiter, not to have to negotiate a menu like a complex one-way system, well why would he imagine you'd willingly grace his hostelry regularly?

As you walk in through the door at Quo Vadis you are greeted as though you have entered the private house of good friends who have invited you for dinner. Don't think the welcome is reserved for us regulars and that we get special treatment, we don't. Everyone gets special treatment. You are swirled past the bar to your table, which awaits you – that in itself is a novel concept in some establishments.

Front-of-house legend Jon Spiteri in his green checkerboard suit comes and has a chat and offers you a drink. As do one of the delightful owners Eddie or Sam Hart, Eddie of the lethal Campari cocktails, winter and summer versions. Good bread arrives, and keeps on arriving, with sweet, cold unsalted butter. If you are awaiting your guest, or dining on your own, you are looked after in a slightly more protective way. If your guest is very late – mine always is – the staff come back and offer drinks, bread, a chat. It may be easier for men, I don't know, but a woman on her own awaiting a late, or very late companion actually feels alone and vulnerable and noticed in a rather disconcerting way. I'd sooner be out the back in the kitchen washing up or have a book to hide behind, because your back-story is being invented by the onlookers, the other diners, I know, I do it myself. I almost ask lone diners to come to my table, it just doesn't seem right. I feel sorry for them. Food, mealtimes, restaurant tables are for sharing. By the time my guest arrives, I have decided whose table I would most like to be invited to, though this minor fantasy has never been fulfilled.

Quo Vadis – QV – has become our 'works canteen' during the writing of this book, my dining companion, Unbound's brilliant John Mitchinson, referred to from now on as 'Ors' – his coinage – or the 'low-rent Orson Welles'.

We take it in turns, about every three weeks, for lunch, to discuss *Smart Tart* and everything related and unrelated to it and life. It started with Ors reading my synopsis over lunch and us putting it up on the Unbound website as the recipe book to succeed my original best-seller *The Art of the Tart*. But everything changed course as dramatically as the Danube a few weeks ago.

Over the Campari reddened with freshly squeezed blood orange (it must've been January or February) and pomegranate juice, and chef Jeremy Lee's compulsory baked salsify wrapped in a buttery, Parmesan strewn 'brik' and baked in the oven, we thrashed out the contents and I went away and started writing something completely different. SO different, that we had to have more Campari and another lunch for me to pluck up courage and say to Ors that it really wasn't turning out to be at all what I'd originally said it would. That I'd better read him a chapter and, by the way, I had NO idea where it was going, no idea at all of any subsequent chapters, no idea whether it would make a book.

And so, over the last two months, I've read Ors one, sometimes two chapters over our pink drink and Jeremy lunch. As winter turned to spring and then to summer, the menu reflected the changing seasons and the querulous first few steps of the book began to take on a life and momentum of their own.

You may think this is the normal way things happen in the world of publishing, but I can assure you, a baker's dozen books later, it really isn't. I can think of contracts being torn up, advances having to be returned, editors calling for rewrites. But in this case, Ors and I are taking the risk, there is no contract, no advance, and, I pray, no apoplectic Ors asking for rewrites. And we have the lovely company of Fortnum's, who have committed both to tarts and *Smart Tart* after – well don't ask, yes, another long lunch and a clutch of subsequent meetings. I had met their CEO Ewan Venters at a Tabasco Club lunch at Locatelli and Ewan and I then had tea at Fortnum's, proper tea, scones, cream, rose petal jam, Welsh rarebit, cakes, and I talked tarts to him.

A book gathers steam like an engine, and you, the writer, the engine driver, just keep heaping on the coals and hoping it'll stay on the tracks and not meet with a stop signal or a hideous diversion. You meet with both, invariably.

After several works canteen lunches, the fourth or fifth chapter elicited a response in Ors that was tangibly different from the preceding ones. We were ploughing our way through a plate of post-cocktail salsify, ox liver stewed sweetly with onions, sticky sweetbreads, fat, crisp chunks of chips, after I had leant in and read Ors the chapter called The Particular Spot. Which happened to be the spot at which I thought the book had finally taken off and I was beginning to get into my stride.

'This is the book you SHOULD be writing now,' Ors said, still smiling. I had sort of felt him smiling as I read, not entirely, though partly because the contents were funny, but because he had got something he hadn't bargained for and that he didn't know he would get until he got it.

As a writer, you only know whether the rhythm of your prose is hitting the harmonics through reading it out loud. I read each chapter to two or three friends first, two of whom are painters, who seem to respond to words directly as though they were seeing a picture for the first time, with no barriers.

Then I read to Ors. I know he knows, as do I, the weak from the strong, what works and what doesn't and he is, ultimately, there to say 'yes' or 'no'. So I choose never to give him the option. I am hideously tough on myself. Even to the point where a whole twenty-page chapter I wrote whilst bussing through the Carpathian Mountains in Transylvania recently was binned when I got home. I started again.

The food arrives and the serving staff deftly spread the plates around my notebook and then Jeremy appears from out of the kitchen in his mountaineering boots for a catch-up. He stops by all the tables. It is not a showy-offy-cheffy bow he takes, he genuinely seems to see the people at his tables as his guests.

It is June. Eddie Hart's new cocktail, the 'Edouardini', Campari, vodka, sugar syrup, lemon juice, soda, a twist, and all sorts of spring vegetables, baby peas and broad beans, fresh ricotta, baked asparagus, the usual Jeremy kind of heaven. The failed chapter has been completely rewritten over a week's torture. Even things that don't work can bed down how you least expect them to then rise back to the surface as something completely different, a process you have to go through not knowing whether you will ever make it work or how.

The Famine chapter felt like the heart of the book and of me, and I had never had an inkling that it was something I was going to write. But the point about this book is that it has been allowed to brew, despite and largely because of the improbably, impossibly tight deadline and the continued process of testing the water with Ors and having him as interlocutor, which has inspired confidence, daring, substance, truth, directness, the best writing I have to offer.

As I have been up and down the graph of despair and hope and attrition that is the lot of the writer, and as *Smart Tart* has begun to shape up, its internal logic become a little more clear, I have actually arrived at the point where I don't want it all to end. But it has to. And who knows if I will have a successor in me, and if I do, when. It is like leaving the best dinner on the plate that has appeared before you and that you didn't order, it just arrived. Which, I suppose, is all that is left now. The habit has formed. Ors and I can't possibly quit while we're ahead. There may be no more readings from the notebook, but there should be plenty more good lunches at the works canteen.

PASTRY

Here is the simple truth. It takes seconds in a food processor, and only minutes by hand, just make sure everything is cold: chilled butter, hands, slab, and work speedily. Then chill the pastry. 30 minutes is fine, longer and it might be too tough to handle straight out of the fridge. It depends on your fridge, mine is American and brilliantly, aggressively cold.

If you are making a 20–24 cm tart, 180g flour to 90g butter works best and you may have a little over for an individual tart or patching or lattice.

Anything smaller and weigh out 120g flour to 60g butter.

Anything bigger, the ratio stays the same, 2:1 flour to butter, just make more. I can comfortably make 450g flour to 225g butter in one fell swoop in my large Magimix if I am on a tart-fest.

I always use unsalted butter and have started using '00' flour for pastry as you don't need to sieve it. Good supermarkets sell it.

ALWAYS preheat a baking sheet in the oven before you start baking your pastry. Woe betide a soggy bottom, you want a uniformly crisp crust. This is the only thing that works. It takes 10–15 minutes to heat up. So:

....

Shortcrust Pastry

Shoot the flour into the Magimix or its equivalent. Add the cold, cubed butter, in small cubes. Pulse the Magi several times briefly, a few seconds a shot, then after 4 or 5 shots, pour in about a tablespoon of really cold water and pulse again until the crumbs cohere into a ball. JUST to that point and no further, overworked pastry is tough and horrid. It may take a little more water.

Immediately remove the ball and flatten it by hitting it on the palm of your hand like an escalope, then place it on a piece of cling film, wrap it and refrigerate for 30 minutes.

Sprinkle the marble or cold work surface with flour, roll your rolling pin in it and roll away from you, picking the pastry up and turning it and making sure surface and pin don't become sticky and remain floury after each roll.

Once the pastry is thin and you can hang it over your pin to fit the greased tart tin, drape it over the tin and ease it in with room to spare. Pastry shrinks, so be generous.

Patch any cracks, it doesn't matter, it often happens. Add if you need to, to the tart

edge if the pastry is not as thick in some places or fails to have come up to the top of the edge. If you have a frill of edge hanging over, just use the rolling pin over the top of the tin and it will roll off.

At this point, you may either return the tin to the fridge to bake later, add your foil and beans to bake blind, or add the mixture if the recipe doesn't include baking blind.

It really is as simple as that.

I normally bake blind for 20 minutes at 180°C/Gas 4. Then I remove the beans and foil, prick the pastry base with a fork so that it doesn't bubble up, brush lightly with a little beaten egg to create colour and a good protective barrier that helps prevent soggy bottoms, and return to the oven for 10 minutes before adding the filling. This dries the pastry out. Note: This last stage is referred to as 'dry out the pastry in the oven' in all the recipes where the tart is baked blind first.

....

Pâté Sucrée (sweet crust)

I make this in exactly the same way as the shortcrust above, but with the following additions. When you shoot the flour and butter in to the Magimix, add 2 tbsps of unrefined icing sugar per 180g/90g pastry and an egg yolk. Pulse briefly before adding the tablespoon of chilled water.

I use Burford Brown eggs, their iron-rich crocus coloured yolks taste as good as they look.

This pastry is less pliable and a little more crumbly to work with, but don't worry, you may just have to press and patch a little bit more rigorously.

....

Pâté Sablée

This is even crumblier, sweeter and more like a shortbread biscuit. Use it if you prefer for any recipe that stipulates pâté sucrée in *Smart Tart*.

For 180g flour add 120g butter, 60g unrefined icing sugar and 2 egg yolks.

Put the butter, sugar and egg yolks into the Magimix and pulse in the usual way before adding the flour and pulsing to a paste. You may need a little longer before rolling the chilled paste out as it is pasty.

....

Puff Pastry

I am assuming you are sensible and have good taste. Buy ready-made, all butter puff pastry from a good supermarket. It is the only way in a home kitchen. DON'T ever buy any pastry that has the words margarine or hydrogenated fat or oil attached.

You may as well not make a tart.

ACKNOWLEDGEMENTS

This book wouldn't have happened or been made beautiful without the following people: Robert Fairer photographer, Jonathan Ragle lighting, both of whom had to endure 23 tarts in two days. They tried everything. We shot 3,000 photographs. They are brilliant and lovely perfectionists and worked insane hours to achieve the results you see, and only the promise of wine and the threat of another tart kept them going. Every shot a dream. Mark Tappin and Simon Gofton who are just lovely to work with and have interpreted the look and design of this book in super-fast super-imaginative ways. Ewan Venters and Tim French of Fortnum & Mason who have taken a mighty bite into *Smart Tart* and become our tart partners. John Broadley who is the talented illustrator, quirky, humorous, brought text together with picture pitch-perfectly. Mark Ecob, super clever cover. Cathy Hurren, crazy-daisy fast copy editor who saw it flash by. Ceramica Blue for lending their exquisite plates. Ors – John Mitchinson – he has his chapter, he has got the better of me and the best of me and there is no-one more adroit at summing up my hazily asked directional questions, act the editor and setting me on the right course. And The Fun. The Lunches. Unbound. For making writers write what they want to write and publishing it, the nerve, the daring, the risk, the edge. What makes the pages turn.

SUBSCRIBERS

Unbound is a new kind of publishing house. Our books are funded directly by readers. This was a very popular idea during the late eighteenth and early nineteenth centuries. Now we have revived it for the internet age. It allows authors to write the books they really want to write and readers to support the writing they would most like to see published.

The names listed below are of readers who have pledged their support and made this book happen. If you'd like to join them, visit: www.unbound.co.uk

Michelle Amos
Paul Arman
Martin Baker
Sarah Baldwin
Juliet Bawden
Emma Bayliss
Moyra Birch
Cat Black
Martin Bosley
Edward Bowyer
Jo Box
Richard W H Bray
Jonathan Burnham
Xander Cansell
John Carnes
Carolyn Cavele
Sarah Cherry
Benjamin Chiad
Obi Chiejina
Rupert Christiansen
Judy Clarke
Kristina Collins
Jacinta Coombes
Alex Courage
Nelius De Groot
Michelle de Villiers
Charlotte Duthie
Martin Eyre
Robert Fairer
Julien Foster
Charles Fox
Ilana Fox
Sarah Frankish
Eleanor Fraser
Margaret Gethin
Sam Ginns
Elaine Gliddon
Ben Gooder

Marilyn Gorman
Patrick Grant
Karen Gray
Jenny Hammerton
Karey Harrison
Meg Hawkins
Tory Heazell
Peter Hirtle
Michael Hobbs
William Hughes
Mike Hunkin
Graham Huntley
David and Jane Kidd
Merci Kilcoyne
Cyril Kinsky
Deborah Spangler Koelling
Chuck Kuan
Johnny Leathers
Theresa Lemieux
Joy Lo Dico
Sophie McAllister
Kate Macdonald
Michael Mates
John Mitchinson
Siobhan Moore
Georgina Morley
Colette Morris
Anthony Newell
NHJ
Malin Nilsson
Dominic Ollerenshaw
Kay Ord
Adam Pepper
Fiona Plunket
Gordon Pollard
Justin Pollard
Sally Prosser
William Read

Deborah Richards
Samuel Rippon
Keith Roberts
Wyn Roberts
Hazel Robertson
Jill Rosenlund
Ruth & Nigel
Bernie Sammon
Christoph Sander
Katharine Rose Sanguinetti
Harry Shearer
Tamsin Shelton
Christoph Sickinger
Heather Simmonite
Douglas Smith
MD Smith
Sarah Smith
Jon Spiteri
Inge Sprawson
Patricia Stone
DA Storey
Joanna Swinnerton
Sarah Thomas
Ian Thompson-Corr
Sarah Tooley
David Tubby
Elizabeth Van Pelt
Jack van Praag
Mary Wall
Jamie Warde-Aldam
Ellen Warner
Alexander Waugh
Nicholas Welsh
Patricia Wheeler
Paula Wills
Benjamin Woodgates
Katie Woodman
Leigh Woolf

INDEX

almond 3, 6, 15, 18, 38, 39, 95, 151
Almond and Crystallised Orange Tart 39
Antipasti Tarts 154
apple 38, 42, 62, 66, 78, 94, 149, 164, 167; pie 47; tart 86
see Simple Apple Tart
apricot 6, 14, 15, 39, 50, 78, 94, 151, 169
see Apricot Tatin
Apricot Tatin 78
artichoke 28, 52
The Art of the Tart 85, 87, 191
asparagus 26, 52, 56, 88, 154, 192
Asparagus and Parmesan Tart 56

Baked Ricotta, Lemon and Vanilla Tart 182
Bakewell Tart 6
basil 52, 103, 121, 137, 154
brownie 15, 18, 104
see Chocolate and Cherry Brownie Tart

celery 42, 43, 103, 132
cheese: Beaufort 137; Comté 137; Crottin 144, 154; goat's cheese 38, 137, 151; Golden Cross goat's cheese 137; Gruyère 121, 137, 140; Montgomery's Cheddar 26; Parmesan 52, 56, 85, 103, 124, 191; ricotta 151, 154, 182, 192; Scarmorza 121; Stilton 38, 43
cherry 15, 18, 90, 95; cherry and almond tart 6
see Chocolate and Cherry Brownie Tart
chives 28, 121
chocolate 13, 14, 15, 47, 104, 176; dark 18, 95, 168; white 38, 95, 151, 158
Chocolate and Cherry Brownie Tart 18
Christmas 28, 35–8, 43, 151
cocoa crust
see White Chocolate and Raspberry Tart with a Cocoa Crust
crab 124, 167
Crab and Caramelised Fennel Tart 124
crème patisserie
see Torta Della Nonna; Strawberry Tart

curd
see Lemon Curd; Passion Fruit Curd
Curd Tarts 22

David, Elizabeth 71, 73, 133
Day Lewis, C. 35–8
Day-Lewis, Daniel 3, 14, 36, 71
Del Conte, Anna 71

Eardley, Joan 115–20

fennel 26, 121, 124
see Crab and Caramelised Fennel Tart; Scarmorza, Fennel and Tomato Tart with Mustard and Gruyère
fig 149–51, 154, 158
Fig, Raspberry and White Chocolate Tart 158
Fisher, M. F. K. 71
Fisher, Rhoda 3–4
Fortnum & Mason 13–15, 22–3, 28, 191
Fortnum's Fountain 13–15

gammon 26
Gammon and Spinach Tart with Montgomery's Cheddar and Seeded Mustard 26
Gray, Patience 71
Grigson, Jane 71, 73, 86, 133

hazelnut 75, 151
see Pear, Hazelnut and Honey Tart
Homity Pies 136
honey 14, 75, 151

Iberico ham 140

jam 3, 6, 13, 39, 94, 164, 167, 191
Jam Tarts 22

leek 137
lemon 22, 39, 62, 66, 72, 75, 87, 90, 94, 119, 134, 151, 158, 168, 169, 192; curd 23; meringue pie 3, 61, 104, 110; tart 86, 89, 182
see Lemon Meringue Pie; Tarte au Citron
Lemon Curd 23
Lemon Meringue Pie 110

McGee, Harold 71
mustard 26, 42, 121, 124

onion 136, 167, 191; red 38, 42, 43, 103, 144; spring 134
orange 14, 38, 39, 151, 164, 191

Passion Fruit Curd 23
pastry 22, 52, 56, 61, 66, 86–8, 94, 95, 131, 133, 134, 151, 196–8; pâté sablée 158, 168, 183, 198; pâté sucrée 18, 121, 168, 183, 198; puff 78, 154; shortcrust 6, 26, 28, 42, 43, 108, 124, 136, 137, 140, 144, 158
Pâté Sablée 198
Pâté Sucrée 198
pear 75, 78
Pear, Hazelnut and Honey Tart 75
Pepper, Adam 140
Primavera Tart 52
Prosciutto 52, 140, 151, 154
Puff Pastry 198
pumpkin 144
see Roast Pumpkin, Goat's Crottin and Sage Tart

quiche 104; Lorraine 86, 89
see Quiche Lorraine
Quiche Lorraine 108
Quo Vadis 190–2

raspberry 3, 6, 22, 23, 88, 95, 151, 158
see Fig, Raspberry and White Chocolate Tart; White Chocolate and Raspberry Tart with a Cocoa Crust
redcurrant glaze 158, 169
Roast Pumpkin, Goat's Crottin and Sage Tart 144
Roden, Claudia 71

sage 38, 42, 144
sausage 38, 42
Sausage Tart 42
Scarmorza, Fennel and Tomato Tart with Mustard and Gruyère 121
Shearer, Charissa 48, 88–9, 116–17, 134, 166
Shearer, Harry 50, 73–4, 88, 95
Shearer, Miranda 86–8, 189
Shortcrust Pastry 196–8

A NOTE ON
THE TYPEFACE

Simple Apple Tart 94
smoked salmon 28
**Smoked Salmon, Artichoke, Sour
    Cream and Chive Tart** 28
sour cream 28
spinach 26, 52
Steingarten, Jeffrey 71
Stilton, Celery and Red Onion Tart 43
strawberry 6, 23, 88, 168, 169
Strawberry Tart 169
sweet crust pastry
    see Pâté Sucrée

Tarte au Citron 90
Tarte a la Rippon 140
tomato 26, 28, 38, 85, 86, 119, 121, 124,
    134, 136, 140, 154: soup 103;
    sauce 104
Torta della Nonna 168
treacle 3, 61–2, 104
    see Treacle Tart
Treacle Tart 66

vanilla 6, 13, 18, 39, 72, 75, 87, 90, 94,
    95, 110, 168, 182, 183

walnut 62, 66, 151, 183
Walnut Tart 183
**White Chocolate and Raspberry Tart
    with a Cocoa Crust** 95
**Wraxall Tart, Leek, Basil, Gruyere
    and Goat's Cheese** 137

This book is set in DTL Fleischman, which was developed by Erhard Kaiser and launched by the Dutch Type Library in 1997. Kaiser's models were the twenty exuberant Baroque typefaces developed by the German-born typographer Joan Michaël Fleischman in Amsterdam in the mid-18th century. Fleischman's fonts with their ornate serifs, fell out of favour during the more restrained and classical fashion of the 19th century, but Kaiser's revival, and the pioneering work of the Dutch Type Library in making previously forgotten typefaces available digitally, have restored Fleischman's rightful place in the history of typography. The modern revival was recently ranked number 37 in the 100 Best Typefaces of All Time by www.fonstshop.com.

Fleischman is also notable for having developed a typeface for musical notation (previously, music publishers had simply engraved musical scores on copper plates). It didn't catch on, but Mozart's father Leopold used it to print the Dutch edition of his influential *Treatise on the Fundamental Principles of Violin Playing* in 1766.